ARMAMENT AND TECHNOLOGY

TANKS AND ARMORED VEHICLES

Illustrations: Octavio Díez Cámara, Acmat, AEROSPATIALE, Celsius Bofors Missiles, EUROMISSILE, IVECO Defense Vehicles Division, KBP, Lohr Industrie, Matra BAe Dynamics, Nissan Motor Ibérica, Patria Vehicles, Raytheon, Renault, Scania, Stewart & Stevenson, Tatra and Texas Instruments.

Production: Lema Publications, S.L.
Editorial Director: Josep M. Parramón Homs
Text: Octavio Díez
Editor: Eva Mª Durán
Coordination: Eduardo Hernández
Translation: Julie Kuppinger
Original Title: Carros y blindados

ISBN 84-95323-28-1

Photocomposition and photomecanics: Novasis, S.A.L.
Barcelona (Spain)
Printed in Spain

ARMAMENT AND TECHNOLOGY

TANKS AND ARMORED VEHICLES

LEMA Publications

The great tension built up between the Western and Eastern defensive blocks in the 1950's and 1960's drove German strategists to develop a very advanced tank, designed to stop a massive invasion from the East.

Keeping this perspective in mind, German engineers conceived and developed the Leopard 2 battle tank which, almost 30 years after its creation, is considered by many to be the best in its class; it is also becoming recognized as the European model after having been adopted by Germany, Switzerland, Sweden, Holland and Spain.

THE MOST ADVANCED MOBILITY

The Leopard 2A5 is considered one of the most efficient platforms of its class thanks to its design and features. It possesses the highest level in all basic aspects necessary for any armored unit: firepower, protection and mobility.

CONSTANT UPDATING

The Leopard 2 family of battle tanks has constantly updated its vehicles since their introduction in 1979. The A6 version with the L55 cannon is the latest modernization presented in 1998.

Ratification of the concept

After abandoning the development of the MBT-70, the decision to develop the Leopard 2 was made. In 1970 the firm of Krauss-Maffei was awarded the developement contract for the new tank. This process bore its first fruit in 1972, with the unveiling of the first prototype that would be followed by 15 more by 1974. In this group an experimental turret was fitted so that various tests could be carried out. Although many of the tanks in this group were similar externally, they did differ in the types of motive power, armament configuration, etc…

Collaboration with the United States

While in the process of ratifying the configuration of the new tank in 1974, an agreement was signed in which Germany and the United States joined forces in order to conceive a new model. As a result, the 2AV (Austere Version, a

simplified version), which consisted of a 120 mm Rheinmetall cannon, was taken to Aberdeen, Maryland for testing, though it was rejected.

This didn't stop the German Army —The Bundeswehr— because, in 1977, it chose this tank and contracted the building of 1,800 units, of which 910 were manufactured by Krauss-Maffei, and the rest by the company MaK. The first production models, which were used for instruction and presentation in academies, were received at the end of 1978. The first of the series was delivered to Munich in October of 1979, with five more being delivered by the end of the year.

Increased production

The factories soon reached the expected production rate, and by 1982 25 per month were being delivered to the German Army.

The demand for additional tanks was so great that, in 1992, when the last tank was delivered a further eight orders had been placed bringing the final number of tanks to 2,125, of which 380 were basic models, which were later transformed to the A2 version; 750 of the AT variant; 300 A3's; 520 A2 models and 175 A5 models.

285 units of the latter model are being updated, starting from older tanks. In June, 1988 one of the new A6 with an L55 mount, was presented to EuroSatory; a model that will be available in the near future.

SPANISH ARMY

Two armored battalions of the Mechanized Brunete 1 are equipped with 108 Leopard 2A4 vehicles, leased by the Germans, will probably be modernized to the A5 standard variant by the Spanish industry.

21st CENTURY

This Leopard 2A4, which was exhibited in June of 1998 in the EuroSatory Salon in Paris, is the most advanced representation of German tanks whose production began in 1978.

European deployment

The reliability and the potential, pointed out by tank drivers from Germany, and other countries, that praised its characteristics, have prolonged sales to various countries, in which Holland (more specifically, the Dutch Army) was the first to participate. In 1979 an order of 445 units was placed, four of which were delivered in 1981.

In August of 1983, the Swiss chose 380 units called Pz87, the majority of which were built under license by Contraves between 1987 and 1993. In June of 1994 the Swedish government contracted for the production of 120 tanks, the delivery of which began in 1997; in addition, 160 were received from Germany to complete the German production.

Spanish request

The Spanish Military's two decades of waiting paid off on November 14, 1994, when an agreement was signed in Noordwijk which revealed Spain's interest in obtaining the Leopard 2, the result of which enabled Spain to lease 108 units of the A4 variant, at that time in service with the Bundeswehr, for a period of five years.

These tanks were transported to the Iberian Peninsula by sea between 1995 and 1996. The two battalions of *Leopardos,* as they were called by the Spanish tank drivers, became part of the resources of the Batallón de

GERMAN MODEL
This drawing shows the distribution and situation of the elements that form the Leopard 2A5, basic details on the German model.

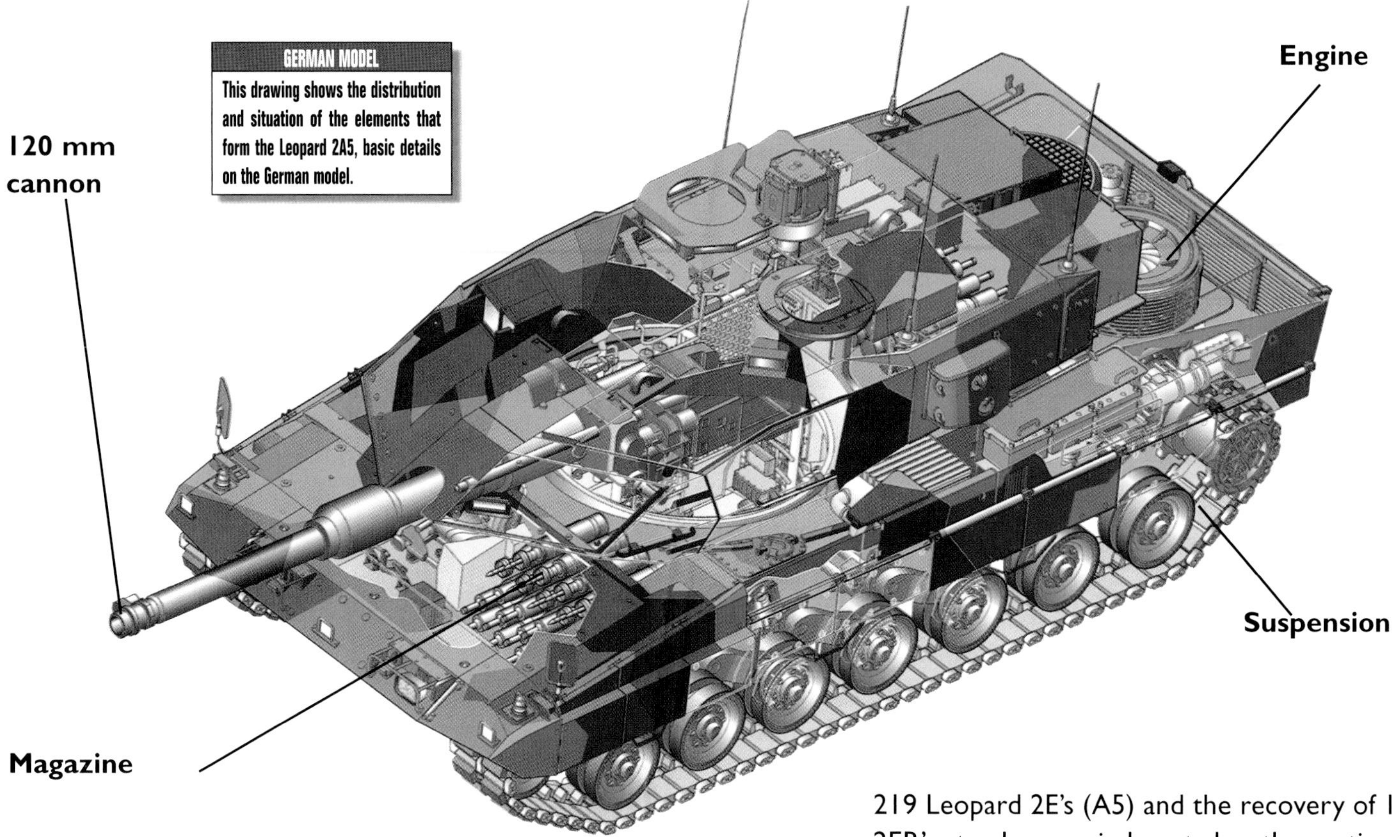

Carros Málaga IV/10 de la Brigada Mecanizada (BRIMZ) or mechanized brigade, Guzmán el Bueno número X, with headquarters in the Base de Cerro Muriano (military base in Cordoba, Spain) and the Batallón de Carros Mérida IV/16 de la BRIMZ Hernán Cortés XI, established in the Base de Botoa (military base in Badajoz, Spain).

This cession was followed by an agreement made by the Spanish Ministry, signed on February 20, 1998, in which the approval of 219 Leopard 2E's (A5) and the recovery of 16 2ER's to be carried out by the national industry, were to be delivered between 2001 and 2006 with a total estimated cost of 317,000,000 pesetas.

OVERCOMING OBSTACLES
The Leopard 2's propulsion produces 1,500 HP that provides it with excellent agility and the capacity to overcome, while advancing, the majority of obstacles its crew members confront, an aspect that provides greater possibilities when on rough terrain.

Firepower

The Leopard 2A5 has a well-conceived combination of the three basic tank elements: mobility, protection and firepower, aspects that have continued evolving in the different units produced up until today.

Powerful and efficient engine

The excellent mobility of the German ironclad ingenuity, that enables the tank to overcome obstacles that other tanks could not, is derived from the high power and strength of its 12-cylinder engine MB 873 Ka-501 MTU engine that produces a maximum of 1,500 HP at 2,600 rpm. It works together with a RENK HSWL 354 hydrokinetic transmission with 4 forward and 2 reverse gears. This enables the tank which weighs close to 70 tons to manoeuvre with agility on all types of terrain, this is in part thanks to the concept of its suspension system, which consists of 7 wheels with shock-absorbers and torsion bars, thus enabling it to attain a maximum speed of 72 km/h forward and 31 km/h in reverse.

Resistant combat design

Although the first units of this model already had a hull and turret made from steel plates, ceramics and other elements to be able to stop all types of projectiles. The latest variation of the A5 has increased its capacity in the frontal arc, which has been redesigned and optimized to face future threats of anything from 120 mm highly explosive projectiles (HEAT) to first generation anti-tank missiles.

Some of the advantageous constituents of these models include excellent mobility that enables fast position changes; a difficult to detect silhouette, four compound batteries and four smoke and anti-personnel grenade launchers.

Unparalleled firepower

This model's capacity, that relies on four men to manipulate its movement and action, is derived from its 120 mm Rheinmetall L44 cannon and two 7.62 x 51 mm MG-3 medium machine guns. The main armament has 42 projectiles, of which the majority are stored in an armored magazine, located in the rear part of the turret. This is designed to explode upwards in the case of impact rather than reaching the crew members. The main armament, which can be substituted by the L55 mount, can fire projectiles at top speeds and distances and works together with an automatic firing control. This control uses a laser rangefinder, in order to measure the distance to the target; stabilized sights, a ballistic calculator that automatically determines the firing parameters, a stabilization platform system in respect to the target, a modular command system and a TCCS control system that connects various subsystems, etc.

GERMAN TANK

The Leopard 2A5 is a high performance model that has inherited the long German tradition of very powerful and efficient armored vehicles and has converted it in the standard upon which other Western and Eastern models are based.

REDUCED SPACE

Despite its large size, the space the three crew members have in the turret is minimal and the loaders, who have to move ammunition of up to 24 kg, carry out the loading of the main armament.

WEGMAN LAUNCHERS

Two quadruple launchers are situated on each side of the tank and are capable of producing enough smoke to hide the tank, as well as anti-personnel grenades that can reach enemy infantries.

FIRING CONTROL

Some of the elements that configure the firing control are located on the right side, such as the stabilized periscope PERI-R17 and the EMES-15 stabilized sight that combine a thermal channel with a laser distance gauge.

SUSPENSION SYSTEM

Configured of seven roadwheels on each side, joined with torsion bars and shock absorbers, the wheels move two Diehl tracks that permit great tactical mobility on all types of terrain.

TOP HATCHES

The top hatches are located on the top part of the turret for the officer in command and the radio operator. There are also various elements used for firing surveillance, all of which are of German design and have very advanced characteristics for the time period in which they were designed.

MAIN GUN

This 120 mm gun, with L44 configuration, is able to easily track, during the day or at night, fast moving targets situated within a radius of 3 km.

ENGINE

Beneath these two circular ventilation grilles there is an excellent 12-cylinder MTU MB 873 Ka-501 turbo-diesel engine whose maximum power is 1,500 HP at 2,600 rpm.

ADVANCED PROTECTION

The sides of the turret and hull are fabricated with special armor made from steel panels, ceramic elements, advanced fibres and plastics; a combination able to stop projectile explosions and anti-tank missiles.

TECHNICAL CHARACTERISTICS OF THE LEOPARD 2A5

COST IN DOLLARS:	**8,000,000**
DIMENSIONS:	
Total length	9.97 m
Hull length	7.72 m
Height	3.00 m
Width	3.74 m
Ground clearance	0.5 m
WEIGHT:	
Prepared for combat	59.7 t
Fuel	1,200 l

ENGINE:	
12-cylinder turbo-diesel MTU MB 873 Ka-501 capable of 1,500 hp at 2,600 rpm	
PERFORMANCE:	
Maximum speed	72 km/h
Range	500 km
Vertical obstacle	1.1 m
Unprepared fording	1 m
Power/weight ratio	25 hp/t

Considered in some sectors as the most technologically advanced tank at the moment, the Leclerc is the fruit of the military industry's special effort to occupy an important sector within the world arms market and, especially, to satisfy the necessities of some of the armies in the Gulf Zone.

This tank, which was created to equip the armored forces of the French Army, incorporates the most sophisticated electronic advances. It has a level of protection envied by many, its silhouette is small enough to be difficultly detected and at the same time only three crew members are needed to operate it.

TROPICALIZED VARIANT

Starting from the base model, a specific variant has been developed, by petition of the United Arab Emirates, for use in deserts, which has shown its ideality for such tasks. It is equipped with a German propulsion group.

FIRING WHILE IN MOTION

The Leclerc battle tank is equipped with a very advanced combat system that allows it to fire, both during the day and at night without stopping, against targets at a distance of 3 km with a high probability of reaching the target.

Rapid development

Since the beginning of service of the AMX-30, the French land units had not received any more advanced tanks even though its industry evaluated new projects like the AMX-32 and the AMX-40. In order to face the challenges of the next century, studies were initiated in the beginning of the 80's on what was then called Principal Combat Engine (Engin Principale du Combat, EPC). The engineers from Ahetier de Construction d'Issy-les-Molineaux completed its definition in 1985.

Conceptual ratification

In order to check the actions of various subsystems, five modules of research and deve-

VERY AGILE

This tropicalized Leclerc, different from the standard variant because of its sandy color and rear anchorage for supplementary vehicles, shows its excellent mobility to overcome all types of gradients and obstacles.

lopment were used that contemplated the suspension, propulsion and weaponry systems. On January 30, 1986 the announcement was made that the final model would be called Leclerc, in honor of the famous French general. That same year the construction of six prototypes, that would be used to validate the results and check performance qualities, was approved. This process began in 1989 with the delivery of the first one, which was presented to the specialized press in the Satory Salón the following year.

The satisfactory tests drove the government to contract, with the firm GIAT Industries, the fabrication of the first units of the series, of which delivery began in the middle of January 1992.

HANDSOME AND SPECTACULAR

The shape, size and color of the Leclerc's camouflage, one of which we can see during the parade of July 12, 1997 in Camp Elise in Paris, are characteristics that make it a very spectacular element, remarkable, as well, because of its advanced devices and basic systems.

Advanced modular production

In order to face the construction challenge of this tank, of which the French plan to incorporate some 400 units (at the moment the have contracted 222), at a pace of 40 per year, GIAT decided to use 6 of its factories. The turret is built in Tarbes and is later installed on the hull at the Roanne factory. In other factorys at Toulousse, Saint-Chamond, Tulle and Bourges, other components, such as the operation system, propulsion, surveillance measures and the main armaments are manufactured.

At the same time as the final deliveries were made to the French, who had reduced

COMBAT COMPARTMENT

The interior of the turret has been optimized so that the crew can carry out their tasks in the most comfortable and effective way possible by situating the different controls and presentation screens conveniently.

their integrated tanks in each of their armoured regiments to 40 (which has 13 units in each squadron and one for regimental control), the United Arab Emirates decided to purchase 436 units, to be delivered between 1994 and 1999. Of these, 388 tanks are the tropicalized model —adapted for use in very high temperatures— which uses a German propulsion plant; the rest are training and recovery vehicles.

Differentiating characteristics

Low silhouette, compact size, automatic loading, advanced self-protection system, excellent agility and the capacity to send and receive information in real time from different sides of the battlefield are some of the characteristics incorporated in this model, that marks an inflexion point in respect to what future models will be.

High firing rate

The Leclerc is equipped with a 120 mm, 52 caliber cannon GIAT CN-120-26 that is loaded by an automatic loader containing 22 rounds that enables the gun to have a firing rate of 12 rounds per minute. The crew numbers are reduced and the gun is also able to deal with a high number of targets.

The main armament's high firing capacity is connected to a totally automatic firing control that comprises a programmable calculator, a stabilized sight system on two axles. The SAGEM HL-60 for the shooter and the SFIM HL-70 for the commander and various presentation screens. Five different targets can be attained in only 35 seconds thanks to the 30 information processors distributed in various places. The firing operation process is reinforced by the control system locators that receive information from other units on the battlefield in real time, therefore allowing crew members to know the meteorological forecast and even the movements of the enemy's units which are captured by satellite.

The 120 mm ammunition APFSDS FI-T, HEAT-MP-FI RDX-TNT and HEAT-TP-FI are designed to equip the tank with the proper destructive capacity needed, and proceedings have been taken to conceptually ratify a new 140 mm FMTA (Future Tank Main Armament) which will prepare the tanks for future medium-term threats that may appear.

IN SERVICE

The French Army, that had foreseen acquiring up to 600 Leclerc tanks, has reduced its number now due to the lack of money. This tank will make up the main force of its armored units and armored vehicles assigned to defend French territory.

Low vulnerability

The engine's 1,500 HP provide the tank with the capacity to reach speeds of 32 km/h in just seconds moving easily at an average speed of 50 km/h on the battlefield. Its downfall is its propulsion plant that emits black smoke that reveals its location. Its movements are very agile thanks to a hydropneumatic suspension that allows it to overcome various types of obstacles and move itself on all types of terrain.

The Leclerc is prepared to stop any type of enemy reaction with its advanced armory, reinforced by its compact, low silhouette. It is constructed from a combination of aluminum, armor plates, ceramic elements and advanced ballistic materials that can stop impacts so they do not reach the crew members. Its complementary self-protection elements are the protection against aggressive NBC's (nuclear, biological and chemical weapons), an extra fast extinguishing system and a GALIX self-protection unit that combines detectors and infrared decoy and smoke launchers.

FRENCH AMMUNITION

The firm GIAT Industries produces specific ammunition to use in the 120 mm Leclerc cannon. Of them are, the APFSDS 120 F1 cartridges, equipped with an armor piecing tungsten projectile; the HEAT-MP 120F1, capable of perforating the heavy simple and triple NATO target, and the inert HEAT-TP 120F1 used for training.

Complementary features

Specific simulation devices have been designed to improve the training of future

REASONABLE AVAILABILITY

A very advanced configuration gives the Leclerc's components reasonable availability.

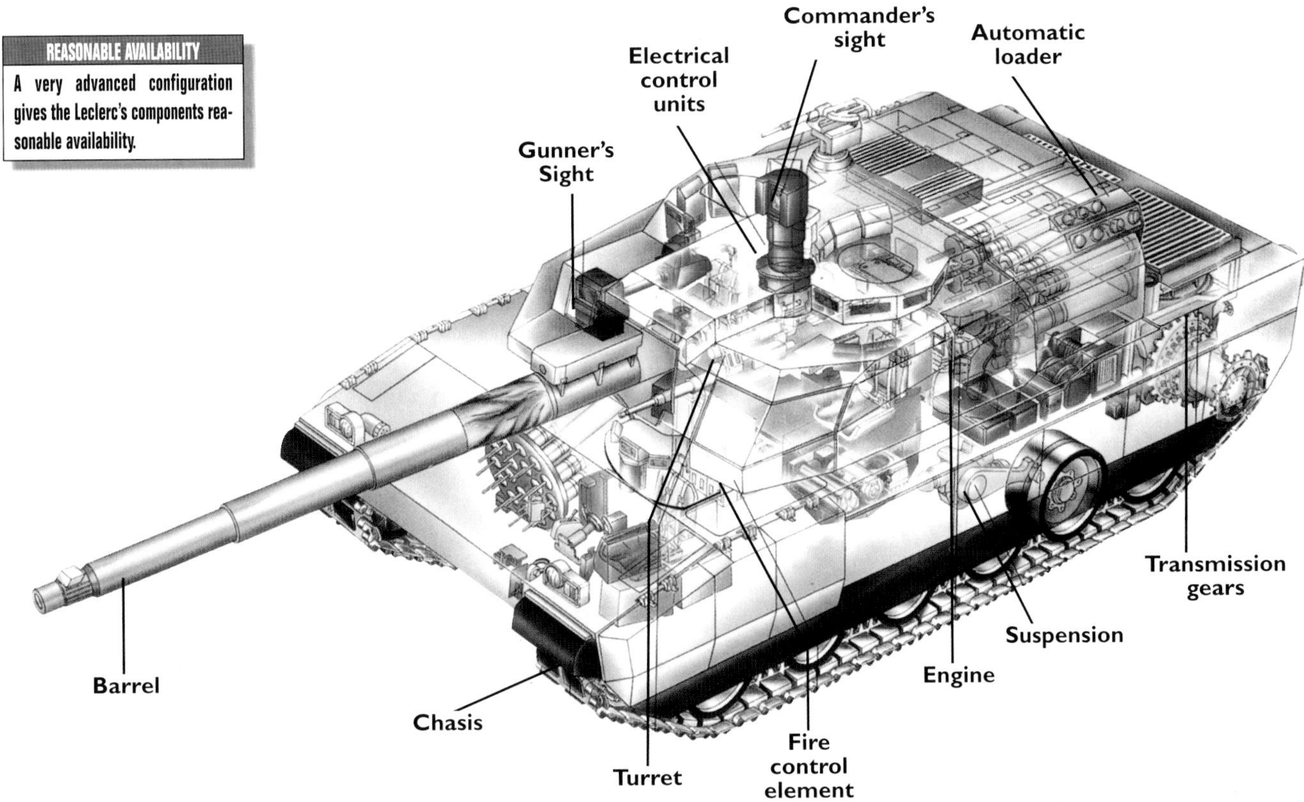

crews and to learn how to use the apparatus and manipulate its different subsystems. Also, there are specific modules for the maintenance crew to learn about the different ways of dealing with possible problems.

In order to maintain the Leclerc completely operative —it is usually stored separately in an inflated airtight turret that enables the control of the interior humidity level and ideal temperature for its complex electronic systems— an integrated logistic support system has been configured which brings together the self-testing unit, aided self-diagnostic elements to quickly locate possible malfunctioning and modular elements that can easily and efficiently be replaced by others, both on the battlefield and in the special maintenance facilities.

CONTRASTED MOBILITY

The propulsion group and the Leclerc wheel system provide it with notable tactical mobility on all types of terrain and when faced with varied obstacles. Also, it has a high strategic mobility that can be increased by the use of auxiliary fuel tanks (see right).

REDUCED SILHOUETTE

The French Leclerc has been designed with shapes and a height that award it a reduced silhouette which makes it difficult to locate on the battlefield. Survival possibilities are therefore increased when faced with different threats (see left).

SELF-DEFENSE SYSTEM

The Leclerc is the first tank to make the Galix self-defense system standards, which includes various laser detectors, the capacity to capture opponents' signals and launchers integrated in the rear part of the turret that can send infrared and electromagnetic flares divert the opponents' projectiles.

AUXILIARY ARMAMENT

Mounted on top of the turret, there is a medium 7.62 x 51 mm caliber machine gun connected to a system that can be controlled from the inside, so as to not expose the operator to enemy fire.

DIESEL ENGINE

Propelled by a SACM UDV 8X Hyperbar 8 cylinder engine with 1,500 HP and 2,500 rpm, the Leclerc is capable of reaching a maximum speed of 50 km/h on rugged terrain.

EXCELLENT MOBILITY

The propulsion group located in the back where, if necessary, two tanks of combustible that increase the vehicle's range by 200 km, can be stored and easily removed when empty.

SOPHISTICATED ARMOR

Various armor elements are located both in the front and on the sides to protect the crew from any possible threats. In addition, the side elements can be removed from the hull to reduce its weight during air transportation or while passing through narrow spaces.

COMMANDER'S SIGHT

The officer in command of the tank has a sophisticated SFIM HL-70 panoramic, stabilized sight available with a laser transmitter with automated surveillance and pursuit features.

CANNON

This tank is equipped with a cannon that is 120 mm in diameter, 52 calibers in length that can shoot its APFSDS projectiles at a speed of over 1,790 m/sec at a rate of almost 12 shots per minute.

BMS DEVICE

The officer in charge of the tank has various presentation screens within reach that point out on the BMS device- in the center- squadron level information. The Leclerc is the only tank in the world to make this system standard in its models.

TECHNICAL CHARACTERISTICS OF THE LECLERC

COST IN DOLLARS:	**10,000,000**
DIMENSIONS:	
Total length	9.87 m
Hull length	8.88 m
Height	2.53 m
Width	3.71 m
Ground clearance	0.5 m
WEIGHT:	
Prepared for combat	54,500 kg

ENGINE:	
SACM UDV 8X Hyperbar 8 cylinder diesel engine that yields 1,500 hp at 2,500 rpm	
PERFORMANCE:	
Maximum speed	71 km/h
Range with interior fuel tanks	550 km
Range with exterior fuel tanks	750 km
Vertical obstacle	1.25 m
Unprepared fording	1 m
Power/weight ratio	27.52 hp/t

The AMX-30 battle tank, of French origin and built in Spain under license, is a first generation design that has been profoundly updated by the Spanish specialized industry to face up to the demands of the 90's. It has a remaining combat capacity to continue in service through the first decade of the 21st century.

Experience, which has given very satisfactory results, has served to verify the integration elements of different origins and to validate the concept of modernization, in which industrial developments from different sources are brought together.

IMPROVED CHARACTERISTICS

The thorough modernization –in which the fire control and new driving plant stand out– that part of the Spanish AMX-30 fleet has been submitted to enables these vehicles to confront, with guaranteed success, other more advanced models.

THE LIGHTEST

The 36.5t weight of the AMX-30EM2 makes it the lightest second-generation tank. It also makes it easier to transport and allows it to cross bridges other heavier tanks cannot.

Forced adoption by circumstance

In March of 1958 the French Army staff granted the company DEFA-AMX a contract to build two prototypes of a new model of tank that would substitute those of US origin in the special armored forces. After its delivery in September 1960 and July 1961, these units were subjected to a complex evaluation process in which its features were compared to those of the German Leopard I. The French decided on their own design and ordered the production of the first 300 units, whose delivery began in 1968.

Spanish necessity

In the middle of the 1960's, the Spanish Army initiated the process of incorporating a new tank model that could improve its armored battalions and cavalry squadrons. The British refusal to authorize sales of the Leopard gun (the 105 mm L7) to Spain —then governed by General Franco— and their pressing needs in the face of possible incidents in the North African Sahara, which was then a Spanish Sovereignty, caused the strategists of the Ministry of the Army to decide on the AMX-30. Nineteen units were ordered of which six were delivered at Irún on November 7,1970, with a 56 caliber CN-105-FI cannon.

Negative experience

The French tank, assigned to the Bakali Battle Tank Company, which was then part of the Saharan Legion Don Juan of Austria deployed to the Saharan Desert, was received with satisfaction because it was new and had a powerful 105 mm cannon. At the time of the purchase, talks were started with the French, about their possible building under license. As a result, the Military Cooperation Agreement was ratified. As a result 180 units were built at the Seville factory of the national company Santa Bárbara de Industrias Militares S.A. in Alcalá de Guadaira — known as Las Canteras; this series was increased by 100 as a result of an agreement made in March 1979.

The AMX-30 tanks that were built in Spain between 1974 and 1983. They soon started to have problems due to the unreliability of the propulsion plant, which contained an Hispano Suiza HS110, 720 HP engine with non-standard features, there was also constant problems with the transmission, clutch and steering. Nevertheless, these aspects did not stop the French company GIAT Industries from producing them. Approximately 2,500 units were acquired by Chile, Cyprus, Greece, Iraq, Kuwait, Nigeria, Qatar, Saudi Arabia, Abu Dhabi and Venezuela, in addition to the French Army –countries that used the tanks, as well as other specialized variants.

Searching for an ideal solution

The poor performance of the Spanish units initiated testing to diminish its deficiencies. Different solutions were tried out from the end of the 1960's, including a Minerva ENC 200 gear change associated with a newly designed power steering. In the 80's different projects arrived. Project 001 included a continental AVDS engine and an Allyson CD-850 6A transmission on a modified chassis; the 002 with a MTU MB-833 Ka-500 engine and ZF4 MP 250 transmission; the 003 was configured with an Allyson CD-850 6A transmission coupled to the original engine; the 004, that only incorporated a German Renk transmission; the 009 contemplated the instalation of a GM-124-71 QTA engine together with an Allyson CD-850-6B transmission and Project Leon that validated the possibility of incorporating the turret of the AMX-30E to a Leopard I model chassis.

Modernization is contracted

After a series of intense testing and examination of the industrial and economical compensation, the Spanish government decided, in the Cabinet on January 2, 1987, to authorize the execution of a program initially estimated at 17,407,000,000 pesetas, in which 150 units of the AMX-30E M2 have been updated. This process has taken six years and has been amplified with the contraction of fire controls, valued at an estimated 9,000,000,000 pesetas. At the same time the Centro de Mantenimiento de Sistemas Acorazados (Center for Armored Systems Maintenance) in Villaverde, Madrid, 149 remaining

EXTERNAL CHANGES

The modernization process of the AMX-30EM2 carries with it different changes in its external elements that distinguish it from other non-improved variants. Among these are the side armor skirts, the transport basket in the rear of the turret and the engine modifications.

AMMUNITION VARIETY

The French firm GIAT offers very ample variety of ammunition for the 105 mm AMX-30 armament, including armor piercing projectiles, highly explosive smoke shells and training shells.

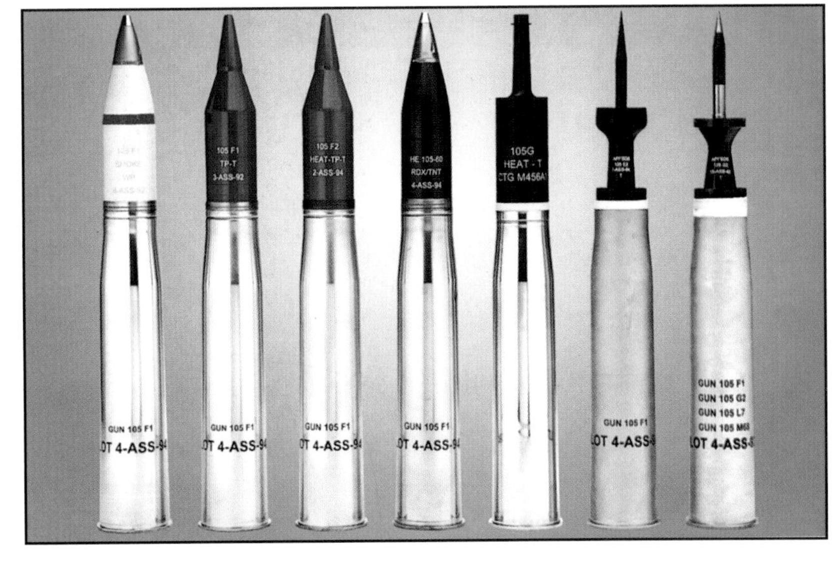

ANTI-TANK WEAPONS ARMOR

The Spanish Army has tested two prototypes of the AMX-30EM2, equipped with reactive armor elements that improve survival in the event of projectile, grenade or missile impact but the lack of money has delayed the program.

tanks were reconstructed to the standard AMX-30ERI at a cost of 6,000,000,000 pesetas, of which a good part have been destroyed as a result of the European reduction of conventional materials agreement.

Technology from various sources

The adopted solution, known as Santa Barbara-Bazan technology, contemplated the substitution of some elements, the improvement of others, the use of equipment formerly not included in the tank and the reconstruction of the fifth Echelon (dismantling completely its 2,500 pieces). This way mobility, firepower and protection were substantially improved.

A propulsion group, made up of a MB-833 Ka-501 German diesel engine, an LSG-300 transmission and a new refrigeration device have been added in order to diminish the original model defects. The engine, made by the Bazan de Construcciones Navales Militares S.A. a national company in its Cartagena factory, licensed by the MTU company (Motoren-und-turbinen-union), yields 850 HP and is a six cylinder, 4-stroke diesel engine. The transmission, designed by the firm ZF (*Zahn-radFabrik*), is automatic and functions hydro-mechanically.

The ability to hit the target on the first shot is reinforced by the Hughes Aircraft

REACTIVE ARMOR

The reactive SABBLIR armor protects the AMX-30EM2 in the front and on the sides. It only takes two hours to place it over the original armor.

CONTRASTED CAPACITY

The armored Spanish Army units have been using the AMX-30 for almost 25 years, although we must keep in mind that the features of an updated EM2 variant are very different from the standard (see left photo).

Company MK-9A/D firing control, fabricated under license by the National Optical Company (ENOSA). This allows shooting a fixed and moving target and its thermal camera is useful in night, as well as day actions. The unit consists of an 8X magnification aiming sight for the shooter; a YAG neodymium laser rangefinder with a range of 200 to 9,999m and 15 m precision, a NSC-800 digital electronic calculator, a presentation panel that can introduce different variables for the shooter, a presentation panel for the tank officer in command and a presentation unit for the loader, through which he knows swhat type of ammunition to use.

Substantially reinforced protection

Survival capacity has been based on the installation of side skirts made from five interchangeable armour plates and rubber. These are able to stop 12.70 x 99 mm caliber projectiles and grenade and howitzer splinters; an anti-explosion Spectronic system that links the combat camera to a Halon 1301 extinguisher to suppress any type of fire in under 100 milliseconds and diminish the effects on the crew members; two quadruple banks from which both smoke screens for self-concealment and anti-personnel grenades can be shot and a TEESS unit that injects diesel oil into the exhaust pipe to create large quantities of smoke.

Likewise, a new reactive module armor plating called SABBLIR has been ratified to stop 105 mm anti-tank missiles. That is why resistance tests have been carried out on two tanks that are no longer in service. The functional validity has also been tested on two other prototype tanks that were finished in 1993.

The space available in the combat turret is minimal and the three men that travel inside have to be very careful not to bump into the multiple devices and systems installed in the interior (see right photo).

The updating that the AMX-30EM2 has undergone gives it a high degree of functional availability, which is a result of the modernization of the majority of its subsystems conserving the hull, the turret and the cannon of the original model.

TECHNICAL CHARACTERISTICS OF THE AMX-30EM2

COST IN DOLLARS:	300,000 the fist series, 500,000 the second and 1,500,000 modernization
DIMENSIONS:	
Total length	9.48 m
Hull length	6.62 m
Height	2.29 m
Width	3.22 m
Ground clearance	0.43 m
WEIGHT:	
Prepared for combat	36.5 t
Fuel	970 l
ENGINE:	
MTU MB-833 Ka-501, 6 cylinder 4-stroke diesel engine with 850 HP	
PERFORMANCE:	
Maximum speed	64 km/h
Range	400 km
Vertical obstacle	0.93 m
Unprepared fording	1.3 m
Power/weight ratio	23.6 hp/t

Additional modifications

Additional changes have been made to configure a tank with similar characteristics to those of the second generation. These changes contemplate redesigning exhaust pipes to reduce the thermal image, modifications to the radio antenna so single tanks cannot be seen, repositioning of the front lights, improvement of the suspension with more efficient shock-absorbers and thicker torsion bars. The addition of a support in the turret for a medium M2 12.70 mm caliber machine gun, modification of the vertical storage of immediate use rounds to adapt them to the ammunition APFSDS, improvement of the driving compartment, etc. 20 modifications have been made to the chassis and 13 to the turret that enable this tank to continue its service in the cavalry units until the beginning of the second decade of the 21st century.

COMBAT DISPOSITION

After some years with minimal features, the AMX-30EM2 has recovered its capacity to combat, faced with various threats; also, because of its size and lightness it is a difficult target for enemy forces to hit.

The T-72 battle tank, of which the Russian Army has 10 units, has been remarkably successful in export sales: it has been exported to 15 countries in Europe, Asia, the Middle East and has appeared in many conflicts in different parts of the world, among which, the recent Chechnya experience stands out.

A simple, low silhouette and a price adapted to the most modest of budgets, this tank has gained respect since it was put into active service and many optimized versions have been produced, thus it continues to be the most powerful offer for many countries.

MODERNIZED MODEL

The Czech industry has considerably updated the T-72's features to satisfy the needs of a new device manifested by its Army; currently, two different configurations have been validated.

UKRAINIAN MODERNIZATION

The Malyshev plant, of the Ukrainian Kharkov Morozoff firm, currently offers a boosted T-72 variant under the designation AG, which integrates a more advanced fire control, a new propulsion group, better protection, etc. This way it attains better mobility and a longer service life.

The alternative to the T-64

The problems detected in the T-64 battle tank were very expensive and complicated, therefore the Soviet designers were driven to think about conceptual changes that were tested during the 1960's and included projects like the Obiekt 167, the Obiekt 167TD and the Obiekt 172. The latter project was carried out and an evolved model, the 172M, appeared in 1970.

Approved and accepted for active service

That same year the manufacturing of the T-72 prototype was completed, a tank equipped with a V-46, 780 HP diesel engine armed with a 125 mm main gun. After various comparative tests with other models already in service, it proved its aptitude as a combat measure, in part by incorporating components that were widely tested in the T-55, T-62 and T-64.

Mass production began in 1972 and the first tanks were delivered the following year to the most modern units, including the Tamanskaya

POWERFUL AND EFFICIENT

Despite the years past since the beginning of service of the first vehicles, the T-72 has proven to be a powerful and efficient tank in the hands of well trained crew members, above all if it has undergone an intense modernization program.

division. Yvon Bourges, the French Defense Minister in his visit to these units in October 1977, had the opportunity to learn about it in more detail and to appreciate its characteristics; shortly afterwards the T-72 was unveiled to the public in the November parade in Red Square in Moscow.

The sales begin

The characteristics of the T-72 and the facility that the countries in the Soviet orbit had to obtain advanced products, quickly sparked exports to different countries. They were used during the Lebanese Conflict where their high vulnerability against Western tanks, driven by expert Israeli drivers, was made clear. In addition, many of them succumbed to attacks by TOW missiles shot from land and helicopter mounts

However, sales of this model continued and today some 20,000 units are made both in the former USSR, India, Poland, Romania and the former Yugoslavia, countries that have been granted licensing.

Other countries that have adopted this model are Algiers, Bulgaria, Cyprus, Cuba, Slovakia, Finland (that has recently acquired many German units), Hungary, India, Iran, Iraq (who built its best offensive unit during the Gulf War where they proved to be Cannon fodder due to the sophisticated Western combat means), Libya, Czech Republic and Syria. Different countries of South America have also

ADVANCED PROTECTION

This detail shows us the disposition of the new active protection modules installed in the turret of the T-72, that have been able to stop all types of projectiles and diminish their effects on the original armor.

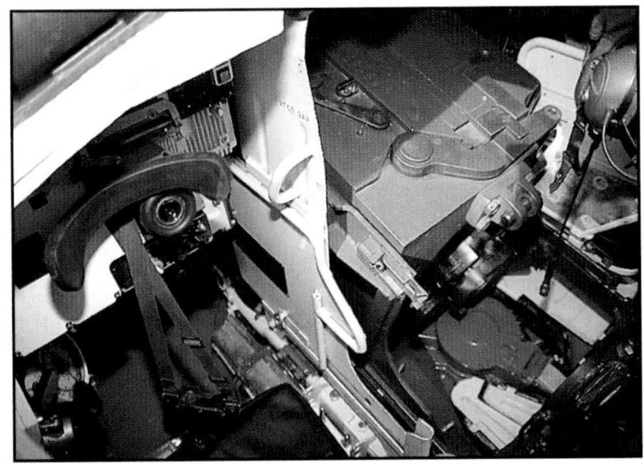

REDUCED SPACE
The T-72 turret is very small and the space that crew members have inside is very small. The gunner and commander who are in charge of firing operations, travel inside.

shown interest in this tank, and they could easily incorporate it given the low market price that various armies' surplus units reached in the market.

Evolved models

Manufacturing experience and use have brought many republics of the former Soviet Union to produce these tanks, under license, and to offer an advanced series of versions that have an acceptable reputation and an affordable price. Evolved from the original T-72, we find the T-72K, designated as a section and squad command; the 1975 T-72 had a low level frontal armor and was the first to be authorized for exportation; the T-72A with a laser distance measure and other small improvements; the T-72M designated for exportation and the MI version of the latter, with increased turret protection; the T-72AV with reactive type armor in 227 boxes fastened to the fuselage; the T-72B, improved version introduced in 1985 and the BM version with Kontakt-5 second generation reactive armor; the M-84, a version made in the former Yugoslavia; the T-72S that the Russian firm Rasvooruzhenier currently promotes as an affordable tank that continues to be built in the Uralvagonzawod plant in the Ural Mountains; and the T-72BU which combines the T-80 firing system with the T-72 chassis that entered in service in 1994 with the 21st motorized division. This last tank has also been known as the T-90 since its standardization in the Russian Army since 1996.

Classic configuration

This model's configuration is conventional: the driving compartment is in the front-center part of the hull, there s a low profile turret where the other crew members travel and the propulsion group is in the rear. The differences between derived models are based on the adoption of firing control systems and the different types of armor.

General characteristics

Excluding the differences in build, the hull is made from armored steel and has upper-frontal reinforcement elements, among which the 8 cm thick side walls and the 23 cm thick robust frontal part stand out. The turret is considered the best of the recent Soviet tanks, it is built (in versions for internal use) with a combination of steel, aluminum, plastic and compound materials like British Cobham armor and its resistance has improved with recent developments.

Located cross-mounted in the rear is the V-12 multi-fuel engine that yields 740 HP, although the latest models have had the V-84 type that provides 100 HP more. The propulsion plant also includes a Synchromesh transmission with a seven-speed gearbox that enables a notable agility on any terrain, a fact that is aided by the excellent wheel system design and an effective suspension system.

MULTINATIONAL IMPROVEMENT
The T-72MP is the result of applying a multinational improvement program to the T-72, in which the propulsion plant is French; the fire control, Italian; the armor, Russian; the extinguishing elements from the United States, etc. This has given it an economical result as well as high quality.

Powerful weaponry

The main armament is configured with a smooth bore 2A46 125 mm cannon –or with a 2A46MI or D-81TM– that has proved to be

TECHNICAL CHARACTERISTICS OF THE T-72

COST IN DOLLARS:	10,000,000	ENGINE:	
DIMENSIONS:		V-84 multi-fuel diesel motor that yields 840 hp at 2,000 rpm	
Total length	9.53 m	PERFORMANCE:	
Hull length	6.95 m	Maximum speed	60 km/h
Height	2.22 m	Range	480 km
Width	3.59 m	Vertical obstacle	0.85 m
Ground clearance	0.49 m	Unprepared fording	1.8 m
WEIGHT:		Power/weight ratio	18.8 hp/t
Prepared for combat	44,500 t		
Fuel	1,000 liters + external tanks		

effective against targets situated under 2 km away. It can fire shells which include the 3VBN17 APFSDS type, the highly explosive 3VBK16, the 3VOF36 with a fragmentation head and the 3VBK17 with a triple power explosive to neutralize modern armor, at a rate of 8 rounds per minute. An automatic loading system has been fitted with a capacity of 24 rounds, a medium PKT 7.62 mm machine gun is used on a coaxial mount and a heavy 12.70 mm NSV is fitted on a mount situated on the top part of the turret. The main armament, which has a small downward range of firing that impedes it from random shooting can be used to shoot various types of shells guided by laser to distances of up to 5 km, as well as anti-tank missiles like the AT-8 and the AT-11 Sniper that reach the target with the support of a fire control system.

Sets used to launch smoke screens an NBC protection system, laser emission detectors and a counter-measure Shtora I infrared system complete the measures disposed to the crew to be successful in their mission.

Models for the next century

The T-72AG model offered by the Ukraine plant Malyshev, located in Kharkov, stands out. This model increases the capacity of the original: It has a last generation fire control that combines a SANOET thermal camera

REACTIVE ARMOR

The incorporation of reactive armor modules to the front part of the glacis and the front top part of the turret, provides the T-72 with a resulting activity higher than expected when the first units were designed.

other dynamic protection elements situated in the front part of the hull, and together with the upper-frontal part of the turret.

This way a high performance machine is attained, which is being introduced in the Czech Republic Army offering notable characteristics that place it, in some aspects, among the most modern Western designs, thus giving it an advantage because of its low price. The only other constraint that faces this program is the economic viability or meeting the standards set by NATO.

and a PNK-4S sight; an improved propulsion unit based on the 6TD 6 cylinder 1,200 hp engine that stands out because of its lower fuel consumption than the original, and it combines new passive protection in the turret and frontal part to improve crew survival, managing to improve the mobility and manipulation and at the same time extending the service life of this armored vehicle.

The representatives of the Czech firm VOP promote, on their own behalf, sales of the T-72CZ. The M4, weighing 48 tons is produced with the notable support of Western industrial firms that want to introduce themselves into the market of the former Soviet satellites. Basically, this model has been improved in areas, such as TURMS fire control system, built in collaboration with the Italian firm Amenia; DITA-97 self-diagnostic and NBV-97 navigation elements; the propulsion plant by NIMDA, with a British Perkins HP-12, 1,000 HP engine and the American Allyson XTG 411-6 transmission; the fire extinguishing system by Kidde and various

THE GULF WAR

This Iraqi example was used in the Gulf War, and currently it is being exhibited in the Nellis Air Force Base. The Maverik missile that appears stuck into its turret shows the ways that these vehicles were destroyed by United States air attack.

125 MM GUN

The main armament of the T-72 family is the smooth bore 2A46 of 125 mm that can shoot a wide range of ammunition including armor piercing projectiles, highly explosive artillery shell, bivalents, etc. Also it can be used to launch guided projectiles and reach objectives with complete precision (see right photo).

WHEEL SYSTEM

The lifted protection panels allow us to se the detailed configuration of the wheel system formed by six side roadwheels, a track that supports 4,278 m on the ground, a ground pressure of 0.90 kg/m2, and a torsion bar suspension (see left photo).

Conceived to face the threats of the Soviet armored formations, the MI stands out for its speed, firepower and capacity to neutralize all types of targets situated within 2 km.

During the Gulf War in 1991 they moved at top speeds along the desert sands, and fought non-stop against Iraqi tanks and armored vehicles. It also reached a high availability level and it showed great combat potential derived from its intrinsic design qualities. The MI Abrams battle tank is the spinal cord of the United States Army and Marine Corps, as well as the armies of countries like Egypt, Saudi Arabia and Kuwait.

MOBILE AND PROTECTED

The materials that the Abrams is made from, the additional armored panels and the shape of the shell and turret are basic elements for combat survival; also the efficiency of its driving system gives it excellent agility on all types of terrain, thus making its acquisition by enemy fire difficult.

Progressive development

After a thorough evaluation of the features and MBT-70 design possibilities, which sprouted from the collaboration between the United States and Germany, the XMI project was decided on to conceive a modern third generation battle tank.

A long gestation process

Along with the approval of the development concept on behalf of the US Defense Secretary in 1973, contacts with the defense industry were made in which an agreement was signed in June 1973 for the production of the validation phase. With the compromise to keep the stipulated price at $507,790 in 1972 per unit built, the Defense Division of the Chrysler Corporation —now known as the Division of Land Systems of the General Dynamics Corporation— and the Detroit Diesel Allison Division of General Motors Corporation were chosen to carry out these studies.

The first company received a contract for 68.1 million dollars and the second for 88 million dollars; both agreed to produce a prototype tank, a chassis and a turret for ballistic tests and a driving group. Once the US Army received the tanks in February of 1976, hard continual operational and engineering tests were carried out for the following two months in order to validate the proposed results.

In November of the same year, the Secretary of the Military announced that Chrys-

ONE OF THE MOST EFFICIENT

Thanks to its features, combat capacity, easy maintenance and tactical possibilities, the Abrams M1A2 is considered on of the best designs of its class, and it has proven its capacity in the many battles in which it intervened during the Gulf War.

ler's concept had been selected to begin the Engineering Development phase, that lasted 3 years and had a budget of 196.2 million dollars and was used to carry out II XMI (X for eXperimental) in their Detroit production plant; the first of which was manufactured in February of 1978 and the last in July.

First units are incorporated

Mass production was ordered, with an initial estimate of 3,312 units at a cost of 4.9 billion dollars. In 1980 work began on the building of different components in the Lima Army Tank Plant in Lima, Ohio, although the final assembly was carried out in the Detroit Arsenal Tank Plant from 1982. At first the production rate was 30 units per month, but in 1982 it was increased to 60 and from January 1984 on, to 70. In February 1984, 2,374 MI tanks had already been manufactured, which were followed by an improved 894 units that were completed in May 1986 when the parallel version M1A1 was formed.

This last version was also interested the Marine Corps to the extent that they placed an order for 221 units, the first of which was received in November of 1990 and the last in 1991. 50 more of these were transferred in the Spring of 1995 from the Military Arsenals. The production of the MI, the M1A1 and MIDU with strengthened armor made from a combination of steel and depleted uranium, were completed in September 1991 when a total of 7,467 units was reached.

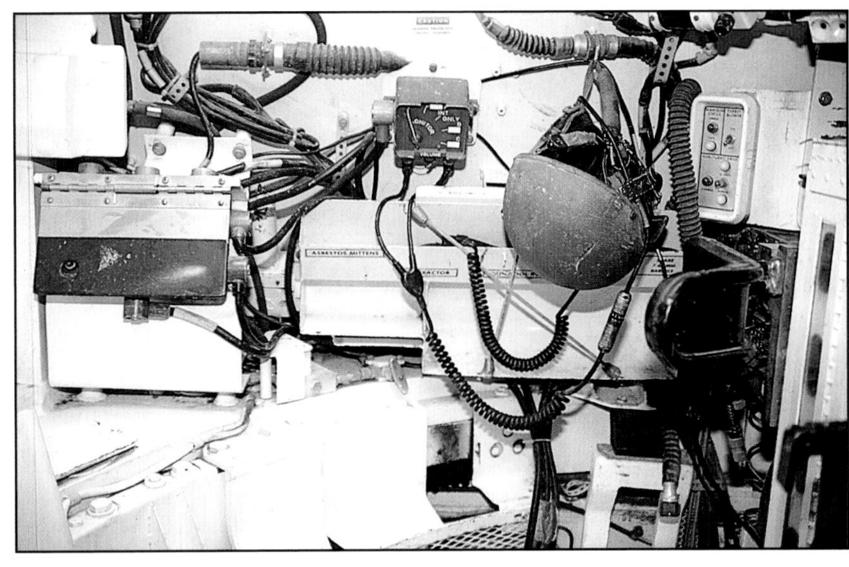

NOTABLE COMFORT

The M1's turret was designed in such a way that its interior has a large space for the crew and different sensors associated to the control of the vehicles; that way the three men that are situated inside can enjoy a certain degree of comfort that is positively reflected on their combat capacity.

IN COMBAT

The baskets located on the rear of the turret are used to fasten and transport various devices and accessories needed for different phases of combat. These elements and reserves guarantee maximum availability of the tank and the crew controlling it.

Improved models

In 1992 delivery of the new MIA2 model, ordered in April 1990, began. Parallel to this process, the Defense Secretary authorized, on December 18, 1992 the first transformation phase of 210 of the MI to the A2 variant. From September 1993 until June 1996, 1,500 units of external auxiliary power were installed which were given the initials EAPU (External Auxiliary Power Unit).

In April of 1994 the improvement of the MI to the A2 configuration was consolidated. Work on a total of 998 units was begun at a rate of 10 vehicles per month, and they were finished in September1996. Around this date, funds to update another 792 tanks were attained, which will hopefully be modernized before the year 2003. Also, since 1994 the configuration of the variant A2 SEP (System Enhancement Package) began.

Exports to the Middle East

The features of this model brought about the signing of a co production with Egypt in 1998, which contemplated the shipment of 25 M1A1 tanks from the United States and the construction of 530 additional tanks in the ETP (Egyptian Tank Plant), located close to Cairo, although this forecast has been increased to 200 more units. Saudi Arabia ordered 315 units of the MIA2 variant, to which they later added 150 more and Kuwait also ordered 218 of these tanks.

CONSTANT UPDATING

Amply modified by its combat results in action, this model allows some details to be appreciated from the latest Abrams variants, that have made notable advances in its tactical operations and firing systems and elements that make up its armor.

An advanced tank with high potential

The basic characteristics of the M1A1 are: a weight of 57.154 tons, 4 man crew, chassis length of 7.918 m and a height of 2.438 m and the possibility to wade 1.219 m unprepared and 1.98 prepared. The M1A2 weighs around two tons more because of the increased protection, although its dimensions are very similar.

Protection and propulsion

The turret and the hull are built with compound armor elements made of steel panels combined with ceramics and other "classified" elements, thus forming a wall that is sufficiently thick to protect, without any difficulties, the effects of superficial explosions of anti-tank missiles, shells fired by other tanks, splinters derived from artillery explosions, grenade and mine impacts and light projectiles, that current battle vehicles are equipped with.

The propulsion group is basically formed by a Lycoming Textron AGT 1500 gas turbine that produces 1,500 HP at a rate of 30,000 rpm and connected to an Allison X-1100-3B automatic transmission with four forward gears and two reverse gears which enables the tank to move at a maximum speed of 67 km/h. An acceleration of 0 to 32 km/h in only 6.8 seconds facilitates fast location changes and allows the Abrams to overcome gradients of 60% and vertical obstacles of 1.066 m. Its range is 465 km thanks to the internal tanks that can store up to 1,907.6 liters of fuel. Its superior traveling capacity is provided by a hydro mechanical system that includes advanced torsion bars.

SURVEILLANCE ELEMENTS

Vision elements associated to surveillance elements are located on the top of the turret; this way the both commander and the gunner can observe various targets and perform their attack with the tank's weapons, during the day or at night and even against moving targets.

Notable combat capacity

An M256, 120 mm gun is the Abrams' main offensive weapon which enables it to destroy other tanks at distances of more than 2.5 km. Also, it is complemented by a heavy Browning M-2HB 12.70 x 99 mm machine gun and two medium M240 machine guns of 7.62 x 51 mm.

A digital fire control that works together with a thermal stabilized sight and infrared TIS (Thermal Imaging System) carries out the pertaining firing calculations; a yag neodymium laser rangefinder measures distances

LONG-TERM STORAGE

The dry, hot climate of Northeastern Texas where Fort Bliss is located facilitates the long-tern storage of these vehicles that are kept in reserve for conflictive situations and can be used quickly and efficiently if the US Armed Forces should need them.

and Kollmorgen 939 sight is provided for auxiliary use. The main armament is stabilized on two axles, associated sensors and a specific design that enable it to fire against moving targets when the tank is moving, something that few tanks can do with elevated impact guarantees and a firing rate of three rounds in fifteen seconds.

ADVANCED VERSIONS

Using the M1 vehicle as a base, many evolved variants are being produced, like the Voverine bridge launcher or some line vehicles that are equipped with the necessary anchors to operate with a mechanical RAMTA plow, that is used to clear and neutralize anti-tank minefields.

TECHNICAL CHARACTERISTICS OF THE M1A1 ABRAMS

COST IN DOLLARS:	5,000,000	Fuel	1,907.6 l
DIMENSIONS:		**ENGINE:**	
Total length	9.828 m	A Textron Lycoming AGT gas turbine that yields 1,500 hp at 30,000 rpm	
Hull length	7.918 m	**PERFORMANCE:**	
Height	2.886 m	Maximum speed	66.77 km/h
Width	3.657 m	Range	465 km
Ground clearance	0.48 m in the center, 0.43 on the sides	Vertical obstacle	1.244 m
WEIGHT:		Unprepared fording	1.219 m
Prepared for combat	57,154 kg	Power/weight ratio	24.5 hp/t

MAIN GUN

In the front part of the 120 mm cannon that arms the M1A1 a collimator sensor enables it to aim with increased precision and guarantees reaching targets at a maximum distance of four km and impact them with armor piercing ammunition like the M829 APFSDS-T that includes a depleted uranium penetrator.

FIRE CONTROL

The fire control of the M1 is totally stabilized and enabled to combat all types of obstacles although the actual tank and the targets are moving. It is one of the most advanced of its kind and stands out because of both its easy to use design and elevated availability rate.

HIGH MOBILITY

The suspension system enables this tank an excellent capacity to absorb different terrain irregularities and to move itself at high speeds to impede counterattack.

THE COMMANDER'S TURRET

Next to the commander's turret there is a mount that permits the aiming and shooting of a heavy M2 12.70 mm caliber machine gun made up of an electric movement system that enables shooting from inside. This arm has a provision of 1,000 rounds that provide it a high range of use.

LOGISTIC CAPACITY

In the rear part of the turret there are baskets for the storage of equipment and airtight boxes for ammunition and supplies.

IFF IDENTIFICATION

During the Gulf War the M1 tanks were prepared with side panels that produced a thermal image that works by orientating its panels, detail that allows the commanders of other vehicles to easily distinguish them from enemies that could present a threat in combat.

PROPULSION PLANT

In the rear part behind these grills there is a Textron Lycoming AGT gas turbine that produces 1,500 HP of power and turns at 30,000 rpm, which gives it highspeed and acceleration at the cost of high fuel consumtion and manteinance requeriments.

IDENTIFICATION MARKS

These side identification marks, used regularly in the Gulf War, distinguish easily and effectively which are the vehicles of one's own army and which are those of the enemy.

Deployed by the armored units of the US Marine Corps (USMC), during Operation Desert Storm in 1991 in order to face the Iraqi invasion of Kuwait, the M60A3 tanks showed that, despite the length of time in active service, they were still able to face all types of threats and to easily destroy Soviet T-72 tanks operated by relatively inexperienced crews. The Israelis continue updating them to this day, because they are considered effective in all types of battle, even though their performance and capacity make them inferior to other more modern designs.

PROVEN EFFECTIVENESS

The US M60A3 tanks have proven over many years of active service, to have a high capacity and a notable effectiveness for combat, although they will need various improvements to continue to be effective in the first decades of the next century.

REDUCED SPACE

This detail allows us to learn about the back of the hull where the driver is located. Its very reduced space limits the crew's comfort and reduces their combat effectiveness.

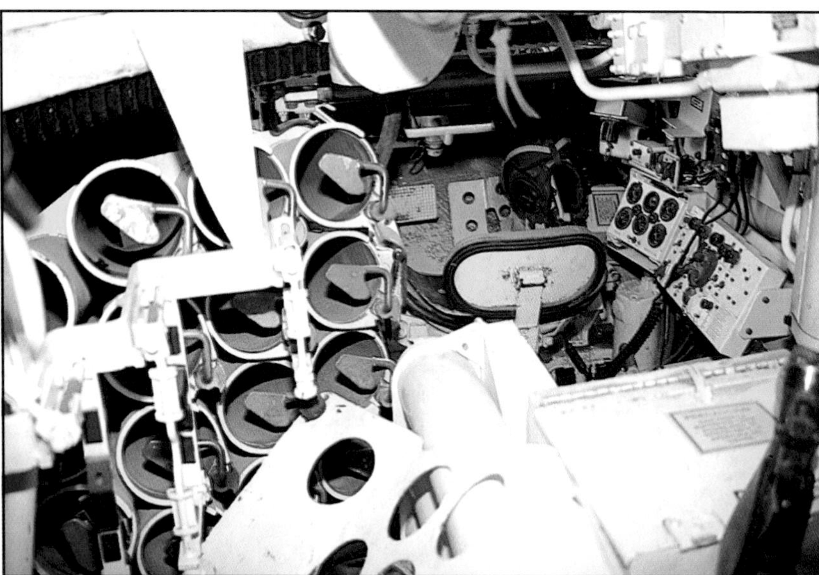

Twenty years of development

When the United States intelligence services alerted their government that the Soviets were developing the T-54 and T-55 family of tanks, the representatives of the US Army found that their M-48 suffered many design defects that reduced its operational capacity. So they decided, in November of 1956, to build a model with better features and combat capacity.

Mass production is started

After two years of testing, many of which took place in the Experiment Area in Aberdeen, the decision was made to start building the XM60 model. This would be manufactured by the Chrysler Corporation in its Delaware plant, a firm that with time, would be renamed the General Dynamics Land Systems. The first tanks were delivered to their units in 1960 and were completed two years later as the A1 variant. This contained a turret that had been completely redesigned and of a larger size to improve the comfort of the crew and to make more space for the equipment and the ammunition.

This model was built for a period of 18 years at a high rate (at times it reached 104 units a month) and continually was improving its different subsystems. In 1973, year in which the Israelis used this model, the construction of 526 M60A2's which had a modified turret with the 152 mm gun from which both projectiles equipped with a fuel pod and anti-tank SHILLELAG missiles were fired.

In 1974 the A1 RISE variant (Reliability Improvement of Selected Equipment program) was introduced, to which, from 1977 onwards, a passive night vision system was incorporated as a complement to the infrared sights M35E1 and AN/VSS-2A. Starting in May 1980, the building of the most efficient A3 was initiated and its production lasted until 1987 by which time some 15,000 variants of the M60 tanks had been produced.

World distribution

A continuous sales policy and other concessions by the United States government has allowed many U.S. defense products to be sold or transferred to countries within its influence when they have been retired from front time service with the U.S. forces.

This, supported by a no cost for favorable countries, has allowed the adoption of this tank

FIRE CONTROL

The M60A3 battle tank includes an advanced system of fire control by laser, thermal camera and primary stabilization that allows firing, even against moving targets, from a 105 mm precise and effective gun.

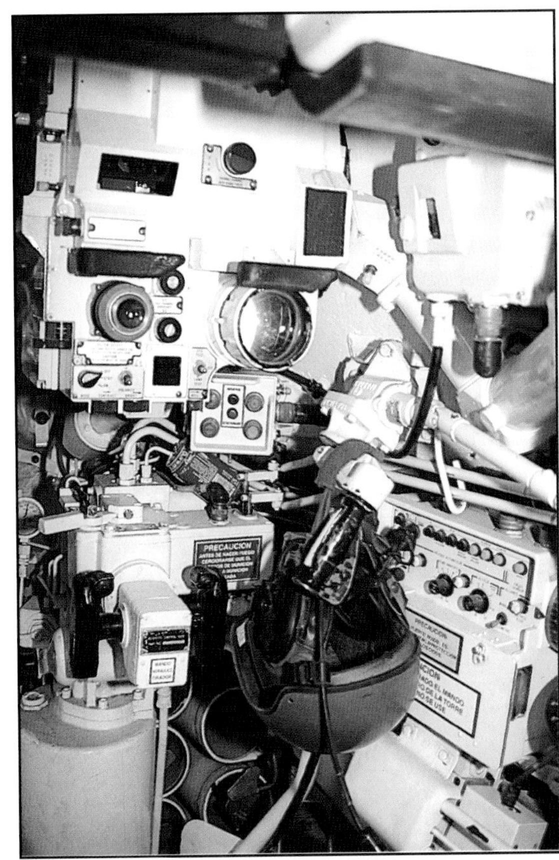

MARINE INFANTRY

The Spanish Marine Infantry uses 17 M60A3 tanks that work together with unloading battalions on necessary jobs to take and consolidate the beachheads; these units have been submitted to thorough revision by the fourth echelon.

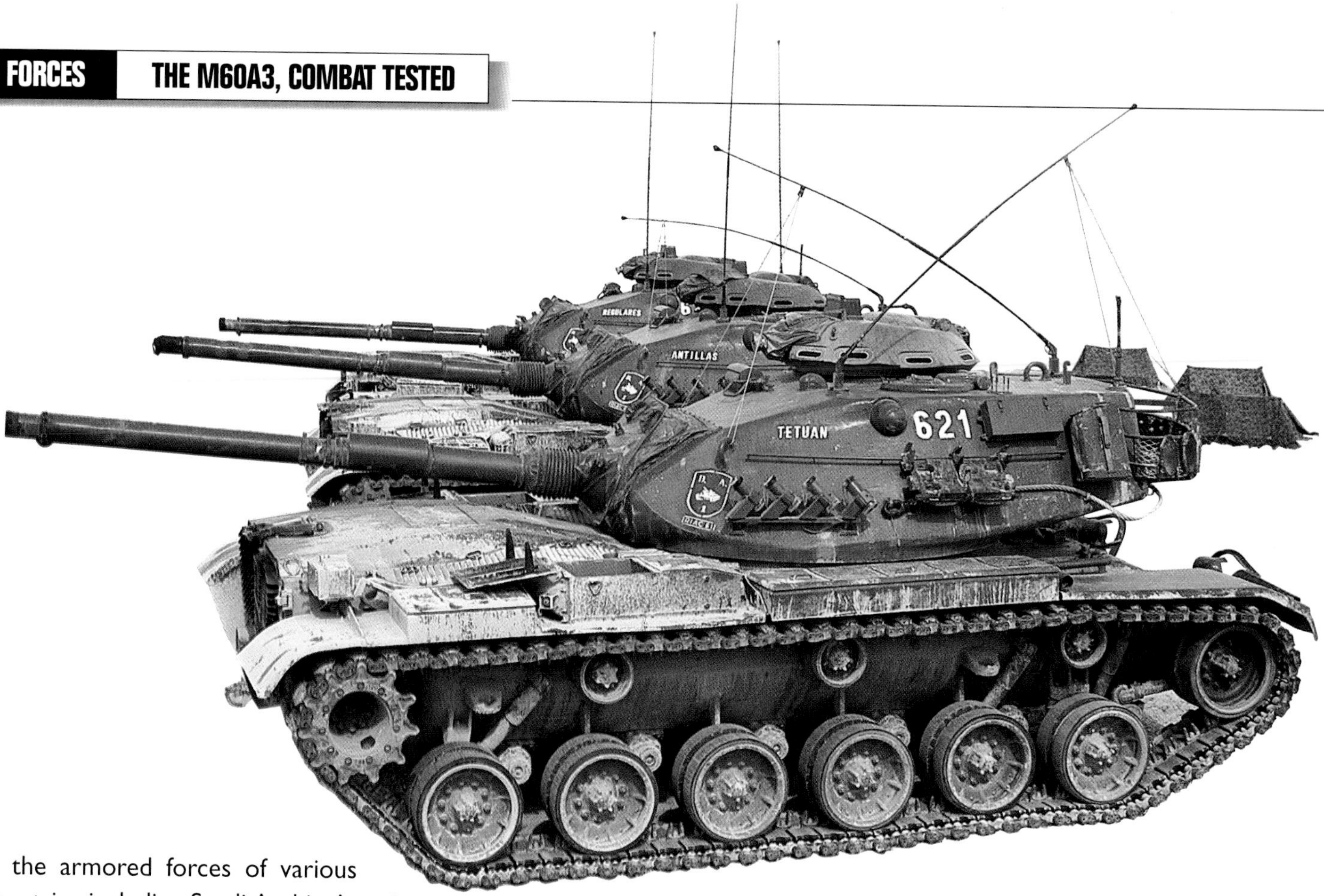

in the armored forces of various countries including Saudi Arabia, Austria, Bahrain, Egypt, Greece, Iran (used widely in its war against Iraq), Israel (acquired some 1,500 units modified by its own industry), Italy (200 built under license), Jordan, Oman, Portugal, Singapore, Sudan, Thailand, Taiwan, Tunisia, Turkey, Yemen and Spain, a country which received 50 A1's and 260 A3's because of the reduction of conventional armament in Europe treaty that allowed them to retire antiquated M47's and M48's.

ARMORED BRIGADE

Almost a hundred M60A3 tanks make up the main armored contingent of the Brigada Acorazada (BRIAC) XII (with a base near Madrid), which is the most powerful unit in the Division Mecanizada Brunete nº 1 of the Spanish Army.

Classic configuration

Due to the period of its initial design, this model has a classic configuration with regard to its hull and turret, which has been built with armor plated steel. A steel that can only resist the impact of low and medium caliber projectiles, and that is able to stop explosions produced in the proximity of the apparatus.

Ready for combat

The incorporation of the 105 mm M68 gun, with which the well trained crew can fire between six and eight rounds per minute, allows the tank to use different types of ammunition which include both armor piercing APFSDS-T type with a tungsten or depleted uranium and the classic highly explosive HEAT type. The magazine capacity is 63 rounds. As a complement to the gun, a medium M85 12.70 x 99 mm machine gun and a light 7.62 mm machine gun coaxial to the main armament, is located in the commander's turret. Both are used as secondary fire and they are also fitted with two banks of smoke launchers on the sides of the turret.

The main combat functions are entrusted to an operational system and a fire control that combine a laser firing control developed by Hughes Aircraft based on the subsystems AN/VG-2 and M21; a system of stabilization for an elevated cannon, aiming and the ability to shoot in motion; and a thermal sight system AN/VSG-2 that some of the A3 varients have, known by the initials TTS (Tank Thermal Sight).

LARGE SIZE

The notable volume and size of the M60A3 tank facilitates its location from long distances; it is, however, painted with camouflage to impede enemy surveillance.

Limited mobility platform

The weight of the tank, which rises to 52,617 kg when prepared for combat, reduces its mobility if we keep in mind that it is propelled by a Continental AVDS-1790-2C diesel engine that only yields 750 HP. This is only sufficient to reach a maximum speed of 48 km/h, reduced to 30 in all-terrain conditions.

However, if its four crew members are familiar with the tank, it can play a satisfactory role because it has a General Motors suspension system and transmission of proven efficiency. We also must keep in mind that very few countries have last generation tanks available in their arsenals. Its remaining power will allow it to stay in active service until well into the next decade, in which surely some modernization to amplify its efficiency and possibilities will be made.

ISRAELI MODERNIZATION

The Israeli firm IMI currently promotes the modernization of the M60A3 to the standard "Sabra" that has a 120 mm cannon, an advanced fire control system, an increased ballistic protection, better propulsion and suspension and a new secondary armament, all for a moderate price.

Israeli experience

The constant combat actions that the Israelis have had to face have driven them to continually, optimize, their resources. In relation to the M60 —one of which had its 115 mm gun perforated by a projectile from a Soviet T-72 tank in a conflict with Syrian forces. Various improvements have been made including the updating of its protection with reactive armor on Blazer ERA models, able to stop Soviet AT-3 *Sagger* anti-tank missiles.

M603A3 TECHNICAL CHARACTERISTICS

COST IN DOLLARS:	**Symbolic: They can be obtained free from the United States surpluses.**
DIMENSIONS:	
Total length	**9.436 m**
Hull length	**6.946 m**
Height	**3.27 m**
Width	**3.631 m**
Ground clearance	**0.45 m**
WEIGHT:	
Prepared for combat	**52,617 kg**
Fuel	**1,420 l**
ENGINE:	
Continental AVDS-1790-2C 12 cylinder 750 HP engine	
PERFORMANCE:	
Maximum speed	**48 km/h**
Range	**480 km**
Vertical obstacle	**0.914 m**
Unprepared fording	**1.22 m**
Power/weight rate	**14.25 hp/t**

Currently models are being made with passive protection on the front and sides of the hull and on the turret known as MAGACH-7.

This concept follows the variant SABRA, sprouted from the M60A3 to which a 120 mm gun has been installed, a totally stabilized fire control system, sight elements for day and night use, an automatic explosion suppression system (in the combat compartment), a spall liner type interior lining that avoids the armor splinters from entering inside, a more powerful version of the engine that provides 900 HP, modular protection elements and complementary arms that include a 60 mm mortar and assault rifles of 7.62 and 5.556 caliber (fastened to mounts on the turret).

This model reaches a total weight of 55 tons when prepared for combat. Its designers from the firm SLAVIN associated with Israel Military Industries, offer this upgrade for two million dollars and they guarantee its ability to successfully face last generation tanks thanks to its increased firepower and armor.

SECONDARY ARMAMENT

In the top part of the hull there is an armored turret for the commander, who has at his disposition an efficient heavy M85 12.70 mm machine gun for use against targets that are not well protected, situated at a radius of no more than 1,500 m (see top photo).

GULF WAR

This M60 from the United States Marine Corps was deployed during combat in Kuwait and Iraq during the Gulf War, a conflict that motivated the installation of reactive armor to improve crew survival.

Specialized versions

Using this model's hull as a base, specialized versions have been configured: field and mine clearing versions prepared with modules of front rollers or radio controlled like the Pele Robotic Israeli. The AVBL with a bridge launcher which works with a hydraulic mechanism to cross trenches of up to 19m, Leguans fabricated in Spain with a sliding bridge of German origin, Bulldozers configured with a M9 frontal shovel, Engineers M728 battle vehicles armed with a short 165 mm M135 gun rounds for demolition field and mine activation. It is also equipped with a hydraulic shovel that allows obstacles to be cleared and to prepare fire positions, and the specific United States Air Force models modified to transport its explosive EOD deactivation teams to the work area.

WITH A FUTURE

The application of a profound modernization process increases the Functional life of the tanks by ten to fifteen, which is much more profitable in countries where low budgets impede the acquisition of more modern models.

Armored forces need a means to aid them in their advancement so that they can perform the complementary actions necessary to complete their main mission: to destroy enemy forces and reach set goals of foreign territory occupation. To be able to carry out their mission, battle tanks are required to have a means of hiding their movements. This has to be completly self-supporting in order to carry out the mission smoothy and efficently.

These actions are entrusted to, in the majority of armies, a series of specialized tanks.

UNLOADING SUPPORT

The British Marine Infantry, known as the Royal Marines, use a Chieftain modified vehicle to support material transport and beachhead vessels; it is considered to be a specialized engineer vehicle.

Launched bridge armored vehicles

Basically, the launched bridge armored vehicle is a mobile armored platform which substitutes the main turret with a mechanical system which works by unfolding and launching another varied length platform, called vanguard bridge or PV, which is placed over the space to cross and functions as a bridge.

The next models, which are known worldwide, have been tested in service for many years: the United States M-60 AVLB (Armored Vehicle Launched Bridge), which unfolds an aluminum bridge; the German Leopard I AVLB Biber; equipped with a sliding bridge that is much more discreet in the launching process and of which Germany incorporated

TECHNICAL CHARACTERISTICS OF THE BUFFALO RECOVERY VEHICLE

COST IN DOLLARS:	**6,000,000**
DIMENSIONS:	
Total length	9.07 m
Height	2.99 m
Width	3.54 m
Ground clearance	0.51 m
WEIGHT:	
Prepared for combat	54.3 t
Fuel	1,620 l
ENGINE:	
MTU MB 873 Ka-501 engine that yields 1,500 HP	
PERFORMANCE:	
Maximum speed	68 km/h
Range	650 km on highways and 325 in rough terrain
Vertical obstacle	0.92 m
Unprepared fording	1.20 m
PERFORMANCE:	
Crew	Commander, driver and operator
Tools	Cutting system, hidraulic crane with 30 t hauling capacity, frontal shovel, Treibmatic TR650/3 main halter with a 33 cable and a secundary halter with 7 mm cable
Armament	MG 3 7.62 mm medium machine gun and smoke grenade launcher

SCISSOR-TYPE BRIDGE LAUNCHER

The M-60AVBL is a first-generation bridge launcher vehicle based on the M-60 chassis, which has substituted the turret by a mechanical device able to launch and retract a scissor-type bridge, its downfall is that it's easy to spot when unfolding.

105 units and Italy 64 units; the British Chieftain AVLB FV4205, that uses the bridge models number 8 and 9. This is basically different in the position of the opening point and in the fact that the first bridge measures 24.3m and the second only 13.4m. The Soviet MTU-72 AVLB has a very original bridge that combines two folding extremities to reduce its length during movements.

The appearance of a new generation of much heavier and more powerful battle tanks, has brought with it a new range of bridge launching tanks adequate for front line use. The weight of these vehicles, at around 60 tons, must be kept in mind so that they can use highway bridges or be moved on trains used to transport civilian vehicles. Among the most efficient models that have been introduced to the market, the German Leguan stands out which, on a Leopard I chassis, has a sliding MLC-70 type platform (Military Load Classe 70, that can support a weight of up to 70 tons), with a total length of 26m; all of which is fruit of the collaboration between Krauss Maffei and MAN. The German firm Mak's experience with the previous company has driven them to recently develop a MBS (Modular Bridge System) that contains a mobile platform from the Leopard 2 on which different bridge models of different fixed lengths of 9.7, 18.7 and 27.7 m can be placed. This system allows it to carry up to three short bridges on the chassis and unfold them while advancing; also, they are able to support tracked vehicles of up to 70 tons and wheeled vehicles of up to 100 tons.

The efficiency and performance of the Leguan have motivated the adoption of two recent models: the United States Wolverine and the Spanish VLPD 26/70E. The first, called by the initials HAB (Heavy Assault Bridge), has been developed between 1994 and 1998 by General Dynamics on an M1 hull. The US Army hopes to modernize a total of 106 old tanks to this standard that will be added to six already contracted ones. The second is a tracked bridge-launching vehicle developed

ENGINEERS' VEHICLE

The German Badger, produced by the firm MaK, was conceived so that engineers could carry out all types of tasks effectively. For this reason the corresponding Leopard 1 chassis was chosen, a notable chassis because of its features and contained weight.

and 12 have been fabricated by the firm Peugeot Talbot España for the engineers. Also, 4,157 million pesetas have been granted to the transformation of a dozen M-60A1 tank chassis, which had been retired, to this model.

Finally, It must be pointed out that the French are updating the Leclerc PTG (*Poseur de Travuere du Génie*), that has a folding UBLE (Universal Bridge Launching Equipment) system, which is a result of the collaboration between the French firm GIAT and the British Vickers Defence Systems.

MODERN AND OLD

GAMESA, taking advantage of old M-47E chassis in service in the Spanish Army, has designed a new ER3 recovery vehicle capable of supporting M-60A3 and Leopard 2 models.

MINEFIELD CLEARING

The Keiler is a German MaK vehicle specialized in clearing minefields, for which it includes a sophisticated mechanical system that provokes the activation of mines before the vehicle passes over them and clears the surrounding area so that other vehicles can safely pass.

Recovery vehicles

The mission of these engineers is to carry out certain tank repairs and to find them in the event of immobilization caused by rough terrain. To do this, they are equipped with a bulldozing shovel, a high performance halter, a high power crane, a towing hook and a platform located in the top rear part, in which a propellant group is usually placed in order to substitute the damaged one in battle. Its crew, of three men, is in charge of carrying out the main missions, such as the recovery of all types of tracked vehicles, towing damaged platforms and lifting the turret to perform various maintenance jobs in the inside, among others.

Many models are made following these premises; of these the German Buffalo ARV (Armored Recovery Vehicle), developed by MaK to satisfy a joint order of the German and Dutch governments, who ordened a model which was based on the Leopard 2. Some of the characteristics of this model include an on-board testing device to show where the damage is on the battle tank which it supports, up to 54 tons. A halter with 180 m of cable that moves at a speed of 16m per minute and a crane that can lift loads of up to 30 tons.

The United States Army still uses the M-88A1E1, an enlarged version of the basic model, developed as a consequence of the modification of the M-60 chassis, although, it

is possible that they may acquire in the future some ARV (Abrams Recovery Vehicles) proposed by General Dynamics. On the other hand, the British still use some 80 units of Challenger recovery and repair vehicles called CR ARRV. The Egyptians have recently decided on the M88A2 Hercules of which 50 units were co-produced.

Finally, one of the latest tanks to be put into service was the M-47ER3, which the company Grupo Auxiliar Metalúrgico S.A. (GAMESA) built, between 1995 and 1996, 22 units at a cost of 1,930,000,000 pesetas. This apparatus required the fabrication of a new casement and the placement of various work elements like a 3.6 m long bulldozing blade or a telescopic crane with the capacity to hoist 22 tons. The version M has been designed to support the M-60A3 version and the L to support the Leopard 2's.

FRENCH TANKS IN SERVICE

Units equipped with the French AMX-30 usually use a specific recovery variant that is called "D" and stands out for its various modifications that allow it to carry out orders.

RECOVERY VEHICLES

The M-60 chassis, which is no longer used in combat, has been used to configure this recovery variant and includes a bulldozing shovel, crane and explosive artifact launcher.

Engineers' tanks

The function of these tanks is to form a part of the engineer companies assigned to the armored and mechanized units. Their main activities, among others, is the removal of obstacles, to perform of all types of tasks that must be done quickly and under protection, destruction of obstacles, hoisting loads, opening and marking gaps, excavating anti-tank pits and personnel trenches.

Among the models in service, the MaK German Badger based on the Leopard I, is noteworthy because of the bulldozing shovel and articulated arm, which is able to use different sized shovels for soil removal. The total weight for this machine is 43 tons and is capable of overcoming gradients of 50 %. The French are working on the Leclerc ARV, which has very advanced characteristics and some proven inherited features of the AMX-30D. This one, currently known as the DNG, appeared as a result of the United Arab Emirates order of 48 units and another more recent order from the French army. It has a sophisticated frontal bulldozer with a multi-

ple plow that enables it to clear minefields and that has rear signaling and artifact launching modules to destruct these fields; it is also capable of dragging a mass of more than 100 tons.

The former Soviet republics continue using a wide variety of tanks that were made, for the most part on the T-72 chassis. Of these tanks is, the IMR-2 , for engineering combat and the PW-LWD variant, for minefield clearing, on which a KMT-6 device can be installed (it can also be installed in other tanks of the same type). The United States has introduced the M-60 CEV Panther which has a radio controlled system to clear minefields. In February 1997 an agreement was signed for the development of the Grizzly engineer tank, based on the M-1. To carry out such a process, 129 million dollars will be invested, and if the features are convincing, hundreds of these tanks will be acquired in the beginning of the next century.

The development of the Spanish Alacrán CZ-10/25E, manufactured by Peugeot Talbot España under an agreement that anticipated the building between 1996 and 1999 of 38 units at a cost of 3,441,000,000 pesetas, is interesting. The M-60A1 has been chosen as a model, although the turret gun has been substituted with a Case Poclain hydraulic retro excavator.

CONTINUED SERVICE

The US M-88 recovery vehicles, of which the Spanish Marines have one, have been in active service for 20 years and have been updated to be able to support the M-1's in their combat movements.

DIABOLIC LOOK

The K20 engineer's vehicle developed by GIAT Industries on the Leclerc base to satisfy various needs in the task of cleaning of minefields, for which mechanical techniques, pyrotechnics and electromagnetics are combined.

The German Army, known as the Bundeswehr, has a long historical tradition of developing and using very high quality armored vehicles that have shown worth in the military conflicts in which they have been involved. This peculiar industrial custom and usage brought the German strategists to design a new compact optimized armored tracked weapon carrier so that the air transportation units could use it without limiting their movements: the Wiesel vehicle was chosen to carry out this special task.

EVACUATION AMBULANCE

The longer chassis and the larger volume of the Wiesel 2 have allowed for the configuration of this specific medical evacuation model in which the medical team travels and injured soldiers can be placed.

ASRAD SYSTEM

The Wiesel 2 caterpillar track vehicle has been chosen to mobilize the ASRAD anti-aircraft missile system configured with an Ozelot platform, quadruple Stinger missile launchers, a Pilkington Thorn ADAT optronics system and an infrared IRST search and follow system.

Peculiar requirements

The air transportation units of different countries have, as a fundamental part of their mission, to move quickly and decisively against all types of targets, during which they usually use helicopters and transportation aircrafts in order to move at great speeds.

Original design

This tank responds to very peculiar objectives in respect to features and compact

LOW PROFILE
The Ericsson Hard 3D installed on the Wiesel 2 caterpillar track is capable of detecting airplanes and helicopters flying at low levels in a radius of twenty kilometers, granting the operator its exact situation in a 3D presentation.

design. They were elaborated by a commission of representatives of the Federal Army. The engineers from Porsche Aktiengesellschaft carried out the design and development of a compact armored tracked weapon carrier whose project, called AWC (Armored Weapon Carrier), was ready in the middle of the 1980's. The Kiel plant of the firm MaK System Gesellschaft was designated as the manufacturer, as well as head of marketing.

The first order of these vehicles, 343 units, was delivered to the Bundeswehr in 1989 and the last in 1992, although at the same time seven more were built for the United States Army who used some of them as radio controlled robotic platforms.

The introduction of the Wiesel, a name assigned because of its agility and operation, brought with it a conceptual and occupational change for air transportation units who could now easily transport it inside heavy CH-53 "Stallion" Army helicopters, and at the same time, it supplemented favorably the features of the Kraka, used until then.

NEW VERSION
In the middle of 1998 we were introduced to met the other member of the Wiesel family: a specific mortar carrier model armed with a 120mm gun and equipped with a low recoil system that allows it to rapidly fire 3 grenades in only 20 seconds.

Two versions

The German order thought of its use as a weapons carrier, as well as its powerful mobility, to provide the necessary fire support to the troops that moved with it. The parallel development of two variants was decided on: the anti-tank TOW and the LAV MK20, equipped with a single-seat which is installed with a Rheinmetall Rh202 20mm gun, which

ANTI-AIRCRAFT DETECTION
Some Wiesels will be delivered to the German Army with an anti-aircraft detection configuration that includes a search and follow radar and a presentation screen on the inside of the armored structure. This allows its operator to get familiar with the situation, direction and speed of the enemy aircraft's tracks.

uses two side loaders that have 60 and 100 rounds of different types placed for immediate use.

The gun can be used in an angle form –10 to +45° vertically and 110° laterally, with manual movement which is controlled by a commander/fired who has a periscope type Zeiss PERI-Z-16 aiming system, to which an optronics system for night use can be associated. The driver completes the crew of this tank that has a maximum length of 3.545 m and is capable of firing on targeting situated in a radius of 2 km and to cause them notable damage, if it is used combining bivalent projectiles.

The specific anti-tank model is equipped with a mount that allows the firing and guiding of guided Hughs TOW 2 long-range missiles, of which five can be transported in the inside of the armored casing and two more on a support for immediate use. The crew comprises of three men, because the shooter, in charge of operating the guiding AN/TAS-4 system with a thermal camera, is accompanied by a loader who loads the containers quickly so that is can fire almost immediately, after the missile has reached or eradicated its target.

PROTECTED TRANSPORTATION
Up to seven soldiers can fit inside the new transport variant of the German Wiesel 2 caterpillar track. It is bigger, which limits its airtransportability to platforms with a sufficiently ample compartment for it to fit inside.

Worldwide evaluations

The land forces worldwide paid attention to this efficient means that could respond to their requeriments, this is why it was evaluated in so many different configurations by Indonesia and the United Arab Emirates, which tried the MK20; Thailand, that validated it with an armed turret of a medium machine gun; Greece and Norway, who evaluated the TOW, and the United States that equipped the acquired units with varied configurations. On the other hand, a few years ago, Spanish interest in acquiring a few units of this tank for the Brigada Paracaidista (Parachute Brigade) was examined.

Interesting features

Its Volkswagen turbo-diesel engine provides it with a maximum power of 86 HP at 4,600 rpm, is capable of reaching a speed of 75 km/h in only 24 seconds; this last detail is remarkable, keeping in mind that the armored mass and the fact that it is propelled with 622 type tracks. The caterpillar tracked suspension system that enables it to pivot on its axle when the parking brake is applied on one of its tracks, is configured with three wheel-guides, a tractor and another large dimension tensor. Its suspension is based on torsion bars and high capacity shock-absorbers.

To its excellent mobility it is necessary to add the fact that its armor panels protect the occupants from assault weapon fire, medium machine guns and grenade splinters; in addi-

tion, its silhouette is very small, which makes it difficult to detect. The fact that its tracks grant it excellent traction, both in mud and dry terrain, is advantageous and permits its operation without restrictions upon different types of terrain. Also, it is small and light enough to be transported in a sling by medium transport helicopters, or in the interior of heavy CH-53 helicopters, where two fit inside, and by Boeing 747 Jumbo in which up to 24 small battle caterpillars of this type can be transported.

Optimized model

The need to satisfy future demands has driven the directors of MaK to conceive an elongated and bigger version that was unveild in 1995.This new model, called the Wiesel 2, continues to lend its ideal characteristics as an air transportation element that at the same time includes the possibility of transporting up to seven men or to mobilize different weapons systems.

Its total length is 3.769 m and its empty weight is 2,600 kg, which rises to 3,600 when prepared for combat. It has armor that protects it from armor piercing 7.62 x 51 mm projectiles and is propelled by an Audi TDI 5 cylinder engine that yields 110 HP and works associated with an automatic ZF4 transmission.

With regard to its new capacity, developments have been made of both a personnel transportation variant and a special model equipped with a heavy 120 mm mortar that works in association with a reduction and recoil system and the ability to fire at a maximum rate of 3 shots in 20 seconds; in their storage compartments up to 30 complete rounds can be stored.

MOBILE LIGHT ARMORED VEHICLE

The features of the Wiesel platform allow the configuration of a wide family of specific variants specialized in the performance of more varied tasks. This unit is a light armored vehicle equipped with HOT long-range missiles.

Its one peculiarity is that it can be operated by three crew members from the inside of the armor that protects them from aggressive NBC's.

A mobile anti-aircraft defense system ASRAD (Atlas Short Range Air Defense) has been developed, based on the Wiesel 2, which used Stinger short range missiles which have been manufactured by Atlas Elektronik to complement a requirement of the German Army who have ordered 52 units.

It is important to point out that this platform is used to mobilize the Syrano robotic project and the German PRIMUS among others.

AIR UNLOADING

A heavy CH-53 "Stallion" helicopter from the German Army functions as a platform for the transportation and positioning of two Wiesels, a TOW 2 and a MK20, assigned to the German airtransportable troops. Its small size, light weight and high firepower stand out.

TECHNICAL CHARACTERISTICS OF THE WIESEL 2

COST IN DOLLARS:	**1,250,000**
DIMENSIONS:	
Total length	3.769 m
Height of hull	1.562 m
Width	1.82 m
Ground clearance	0.302 m
WEIGHTS:	
Empty	2,600 kg
Prepared for combat	3,600 kg
Fuel	120 l

ENGINE:	
Audi turbo-diesel direct injection 5 cylinder 110 hp	
PERFORMANCE:	
Maximum speed	70 km/h
Range	550 km
Power/weight ratio	30.5 hp/t

SENSORS

The group of integrated sensors in this mount consist of a television camera to observe during the day what happens at long distances; a laser rangefinder to measure the exact position of the targets, and a thermal camera to allow vision at night or in adverse conditions.

DETAILED REAR

The rear part of the Wiesel integrates a door that allows the crew to access the inside. Rear marking elements are located in this area and tools that are used in auxiliary tasks.

EFFICIENT SUSPENSION SYSTEM

Wiesel vehicles include a suspension system with three roadwheels, a front drive sprocket and a rear tensor that move 622 type tracks moving the vehicle on all types of terrain.

FIREPOWER

This ammunition box has the capacity to store 100 20 mm rounds cartridges that are moved by a mechanical belt to a tense shot cannon chamber. The left side container corresponds to a long-range anti-tank missile and high capacity Euromissile HOT.

WEAPON RECONNAISSANCE

This reconnaissance variant contains a hydraulic mast that raises the sensor group so as to observe, without being seen, a fast shot 20mm cannon and a launcher to fire anti-tank HOT missiles. Its capacity is superior to those in its class.

ENGINE

This vehicle has a Volkswagen turbo-diesel motor that has 86 HP at 4,500 rpm. It is connected to an automatic ZF 3HP22 3 speed transmission that moves it at a maximum 75 km/h.

INCLINED FRONT

The front panels are inclined so as to provide a greater resistance to all types of impacts. On the left, below these is the engine that can be accessed by a special hatch. The driver is on the right side where the three periscopes for exterior surveillance are located.

The need for modern combat vehicles caused the Spanish military to look at the possibility of developing a new model, on the basis of the country's own industrial capacity, although it did resort to exterior technological support.

This process, which has been carried out together with the Austrian firm Steryr-Daimler-Puch Spezialfahrzeug AG, has given rise to the model internationally known as ASCOD (Austrian-Spanish Cooperative Development); to date 114 units have already been acquired by the Spanish Army, where it is called "Pizarro" and it is soon to be incorporated in the Cavalry and Infantry units.

OPERATIONAL IN 1999

The Spanish Army has ordered the production of the first 144 units of the Pizarro series, vehicles that will begin to arrive to the División Mecanizada "Brunete" nº 1 in 1999 to replace the old TOA M-113 of its infantry battalions.

LONG DEVELOPMENT

It has taken fifteen years to perfect the VCI Pizarro, that will equip the Spanish and Austrian mechanized units.

Accidental development

In the end of 1984 a commission of experts in charge of studying and defining the basic characteristics of a combat vehicle VCI/C (Infantry/Cavalry Combat Vehicle), was created to empower the capacity of various units of the Spanish Army and to substitute, in the medium-term, the thousand United States armored vehicles of the M-113 family that were divided among different bases.

Work is begun

The Armored Division (División de Blindados) of the Empresa Nacional de Autocamiones S.A. (ENASA), also known by the name Pegaso, which had prior experience in the design and building of armored vehicles and had already been given the job of producing the BMR and VEC wheels, was chosen to carry out this arduous task.

The firm's engineers began experimenting different configurations and working with elements that would configure the vehicle. They tried a Pegaso reinforced engine that could produce the 505 hp necessary to move the VCI. Following the first studies, the Valladolid firm was taken over by the Italian IVECO com-

pany that took control of the development of the Nacional Santa Bárbara which absorbed the Armored Divison.

The project is consolidated

The first phase of development was followed by a second, much more ambitious phase. This contemplated the new operative requirements manifested in 1988 by the military personnel for better features. The difficulties came out in this process, and the impossibility to reach significant advances brought about a signed agreement with the Austrian company Steyr. They contemplated the production of joint works, with the aim of achieving a much more advanced vehicle capable of being exported to other countries, with the two countries sharing possible markets in their area of influence.

In 1991 the prototype PT-1 was ready. It was submitted to a long series of tests in August of the same year at the Sevillian Las Canteras and the Cádiz Costilla camps. Later it was transported by a C-130H plane, "Hércules", to Norway to be evaluated there in the hard climatic conditions of the Arctic Circle.

The improvements asked for by the Norwegian Army obligated the building of a second prototype this still presented maneuvering problems in deep snow. A third was decided on and evaluated in Austria during the Summer of 1993. The PT-4 followed the latter with a lengthened suspension system that has been extensively tested in Spain, where it has found good mobility, efficiency and firepower similar to those proposed by other countries. All of this has led to a contract of 4 units that will be followed by 366 more vehicles to be be delivered in installments between 1999 and 2005.

REACTIVE ARMOR

Thought has been given to the implementation of frontal protection based on various reactive or ceramic configurations of reduced weight and increased resistance of all types of impacts.

EVACUATION PROTOTYPE

The performance tests have obligated the construction of four prototypes, designated PT-1 to PT-4, that have been submitted to a rigorous feature validation process.

PRODUCTIVE SELF-SUFFICIENCY

The Spanish capacity to produce, together with the Austrian firm Steyr, a high performance armored caterpillar track combat vehicle is an important milestone in regards to maintaining and boosting the defense industry's capacity to face challenges of all sizes.

Very advanced vehicles

The ability to resist 30 mm armor piercing projectiles, gives the crew increased security when faced with various combat situations.The Pizarro is outstanding for its low silhouette, reduced size and extraordinary mobility; aspects that satisfy the tactical necessities of any current armored formation.

Multinational configuration

The hull has a classic configuration with the engine and driver in its front part, the turret in the center and in the rear the infantry transportation compartment. Built with steel armor panels of different thicknesses —that can be reinforced with reactive Santa Bárbara SABBLIR system elements— various motive elements are located in the hull. They include the two lateral track systems with seven support wheels, torsion bars and shock-absorbers in the first and the sixth wheel, and a MTU diesel engine that yields 600 HP and a hydraulic-mechanical Renk HSWL 106 automatic 6 gear transmission.

The transportation area includes various top hatches for surveillance and evacuation and an ample rear hatch to quickly abandon the vehicle. It is also equipped with additional security elements like the anti-explosion system and a spall liner that avoids chipping of the armor towards the inside upon external impact. It also includes an air filter system to be able to combat in situations where aggressive NBC's have been detected.

POWERFUL AND EFFICIENT

The ASCOD family contemplated various vehicles configured as light armored vehicles to substitute the original turret for a South African LTM equipped with a 105 mm low recoil gun. It has a remarkable capacity to resist 23 mm impacts on its frontal arc.

Combat vehicle

The variant VCI/VCC (Combat Vehicle) includes a two-seat turret made of armor plates that integrates a German Mauser Mk30 totally stabilized automatic gun, that fires powerful 30 x 173 mm ammunition at a high rate and includes a 400 round reserve, of which 200 are in the arm's loaders.

As a complement of the arm, it has a medium MG-42/58 machine gun, on a coaxial mount, that fires its 7.62 x 51 mm ammunition at a rate of 800 rounds per minute, and at the same time the sextuple sets of smoke and anti-personnel grenade launchers are located on the sides of the turret.

The vehicle's commander and the gunner, rely on top hatches for access and evacuation, have an MK10 ENOSA (Empresa Nacional de Óptica S.A.) digital shooting control at their disposal configured for a ballistic calculator that receives data from various sensor panels, a laser distance measurer to know the distances of the targets, a thermal camera for both day and night vision and the different control and activation units. To complement

this, there are 15 surveillance periscopes that enable complete exterior vision.

VERY MOBILE PLATFORM

The configuration of the propulsion group and the features of the caterpillar track enable the ASCOD to overcome any type of obstacle, reaching a very high speed on all types of terrain.

Family with a future

Using the hull as the basis of this vehicle, work has already been started on the construction of two national models to complement more specific activities. The first variation, already contracted by the Spanish Army, is in the control area. It has an identical exterior to that of the battle tank and has substantially modified the personnel compartment to place additional transmission devices, tables, map carrier, etc..

The other model is being experimented on and is similar to the light tank or fire support vehicle that was unveiled in June 1998 in Paris. It includes a sophisticated South African LMT-105 turret that has a 105 mm low recoil gun with a fire control that allows aiming and firing while the tank is in movement; all of this at a weight of 6.5 tons.

In the future, the birth of other variants is expected that will include a light armored vehicle with a TOW anti-tank missile mount, a rocket-launcher with a Teruel system module, a mortar carrier with a 120 mm gun, an anti-aircraft defense vehicle with a turret that will combine cannons and missiles, a recovery vehicle, a transmission vehicle, a self-propelled artillery gun with a 155 mm mount and a long etcetera of specialized vehicles.

LIGHT ARMORED VEHICLE

The Spanish-Austrian ASCOD is equipped with a LMT-105 South African turret of 6.5t to verify its capacity as a light armored vehicle. Its tactical mobility and features that allow it to hit targets on the first shot are noteworthy.

FIRE CONTROL

The ENOSA MK10 system is a very modern fire control that allows the Pizarro crew to combat both during the day and at night with the possibility of using the 30 mm main gun when the vehicle is in motion.

TWO-SEATED TURRET

The two-seated Pizarro turret is configured with thick walls that are resistant to the impact of projectiles of up to 30 mm caliber and it is equipped with a Mauser 30 mm cannon and has various additional equipment like the MK10 digital fire control system or the grenade.

PROPULSION GROUP

The engine that propels the Pizarro family is a German diesel MTU v-8 183 TE22 v-90 that yields 600 HP at 2,300 rpm and works associated with a Renk HSWL 106 hydromechanical 6 gear transmission.

TOP DETAIL

The driver is located in the top left part of the frontal area and has an armored turret and surveillance sights. The propulsion group is located on the right side, which can be accessed through a protective ventilation grate.

SUSPENSION SYSTEM

The suspension system is configured with seven roadwheels, the idler wheel and the drive sprocket that move two tracks with links that produce a ground pressure of 0.62 kg/cm^2. The suspension is through torsion bars and shock-absorbers.

RESERVE BOXES

Two enormous metallic boxes are located in the rear part of the vehicle that are used to transport various additional equipment, that can also be configured as supplementary tanks or to place the air filter units in polluted areas.

SURVEILLANCE TURRET

A circular turret is located in the personnel transportation area that includes various periscopes so that the transported soldiers can see what is happening around it. This can be used to evacuate the vehicle in case of damage to the rear hatch.

TRANSPORTATION AREA

The rear part of the Pizzaro integrates a folding ramp that allows the soldiers to load and unload the vehicle. The six soldiers of the squad sit in individual seats that improve their comfort in difficult movement on all types of terrain.

TECHNICAL CHARACTERISTICS OF THE VCI PIZARRO

COST IN DOLLARS:	**1,500,000**
DIMENSIONS:	
Total length	6.224 m
Height	2.653 m
Width	3.002 m
Ground clearance	0.45 m
WEIGHTS:	
Prepared for combat	25,200 kg
Fuel	650 l

ENGINE:	
Diesel MTU BV 183 TE22 V-90 8 cylinder engine that yields 600 HP at 2,300 rpm	
FEATURES:	
Maximum speed	70 km/h
Range	600 km
Vertical target range	0.95 m
Transport capacity	3 crew members & 8 soldiers
Unprepared fording	1.2 m
Power/weight ratio	23.8 hp/t

The Stridsfordon 90 (CV, Combat Vehicle) was brought about to meet the requirements of the Swedish Armed Forces. It has become one of the most advanced models in its category and has given rise to a very wide family of specific variants, that are manufactured both for the Swedish and Norwegian armies.

Its stealthy shapes, stylish design, integral NBC protection, efficient extinguishing system, low level of thermal radiation and its general capabilities has made this tank one by which all others are judged. It has been proven in all types of tests –some of which took place in the Arctic Circle– its mobility and ability to face the most varied climatological conditions, keeping intact its fighting readiness.

COMBAT VEHICLE
This CV 9030 stands out because it is armed with a rapid firing Bushmaster II 30mm that allows different fixed and moving targets to be hit and to face all types of armored vehicles or tanks.

OPTIMIZED DESIGN
The CV 90 family has been optimized in various aspects of conception, operation and maintenance.

Productive self-sufficiency

Sweden has maintained productive self-sufficiency in many areas which has driven its own defense industry to face the most difficult of tasks, such as combat aircrafts, ships and submarines.

To this end, the Swedish Army proposed and developed a new tracked infantry combat vehicle which contained the features they considered such a vehicle should have. It received the initial designation of CV 90.

Satisfactory development

Keeping in mind very advanced protection, mobility and firepower features, Hägglunds Vehicle Ab, situated in the town of Örnsköldsvik, started various studies that benefited from their prior experience in the development of vehicles like the Bv-206 mountain caterpillar.

These projects were started in 1984 after signing a development contract with the Swedish Defense Material Administration (FMV). It included the collaboration of the Bofors company, as far as the contribution of the

armament and turret were concerned. First the hull was built for driving tests and later five validation vehicles were built in order to test different turret models. The differences between the models was based on the movement systems (manual, hydraulic or electric) and the caliber of the armament, of 25 or 40 millimeters.

DESIGN DETAILS

In the front part of a CV 90 ARV we can see the ripper shovel that can be used to move obstacles, land or vehicles, and is very useful for the recovery assignments given by the Swedish Army who has it in service.

Although 30,000,000,000 pesetas were invested in its development, commercial elements already tested were agreed upon to reduce production costs. Its acquisition was decided upon after signing the contract in March 1991.

Deliveries begin

The first CV 9040 —these last numbers identify the caliber of the armament— were delivered to the Army on November 1, 1993. A few months before an agreement was signed for the development of four more variants, one of which was a specific anti-aircraft defense model, one for advanced surveillance, one for control and one for recovery that, respectively, were given the names TriAD, CV 90 FOV, CV 90 FCV and CV 90 ARV.

In April, 1994, the FMV placed an order for 150 additional CV 90 units, raising the number of ordered vehicles for the Swedish mechanized brigades to around 600. That same month, news was given of the Norwegian Army's choice of the armored CV 9030N that was extensively evaluated together with the Spanish-Austrian ASCOD and the United States M-2 Bradley. The order was a total of 104 units, delivered between 1995 and 1997.

Optimized variants

To complement the basic CV 9040 model –the improved CV 9040A model has been produced and the 9040B is under construction for delivery in 1999– this will use a L70 40 mm gun and satisfy both their own needs and those derived from a clear intention to obtain a new export contract. Hägglunds has actively worked on the conception and brought adapted combat possibilities to perfection, including the CV 9025 model, equipped with a Bushmaster or Mauser 25 mm gun and the CV 9030, armed with a 30 mm Bushmaster II.

If increased firepower with anti-tank capability is sought, the CV 901905 should be used because it is equipped with the French GIAT company's TML turret with a stabilized 105 mm mount and prepared with day and night vision elements, which can be installed on other similar or more powerful turrets to

TECHNICAL CHARACTERISTICS OF THE CV 9040T

COST IN DOLLARS	**2,600,000**
DIMENSIONS:	
Hull length	6.471 m
Height	2.5 m
Width	3.01 m
Ground clearance	0.45 m
WEIGHTS:	
Prepared for combat	22,800 kg
Fuel	525 l
ENGINE:	
Diesel Scania DS14 550 hp engine	

FEATURES:	
Maximum speed	70 km/h
Range	300 km
Vertical obstacle	0.60 m
Trench crossing	2.50 m
Power/weight ratio	2.12 hp/t
FEATURES:	
Transport capacity	3 crew members and 8 soldiers
Ground pressure	0.53 kg/cm²

configure the CV 90120. The anti-aircraft function is bestowed to the CV 9040 AAV, that connects the basic model turret to radar capable of detecting aircraft within a 4 km radius and an automatic evaluation system of potential threats. The CV 90 FOV is used to observe the enemy's movements and is equipped with navigation system and a laser measurement device to reach targets and improve communication. The CV 90 FCV is configured as a mobile command and control station (C2) in which the best staff elements work; while the CV 90 ARV includes a bulldozer, crane and other elements that enable the recovery of up to 72 tons.

Good performance

The increased mobility and low inherent ground pressure of its propulsion group, very low maintenance and operational costs, the ability to be stored for long periods of time with an increased availability and the capacity of the integrated systems, for combat both during the day and at night this give the CV 90 family many possibilities that favorably distinguish it from other contemporary designs that have not advanced as consecutively in regards to possibilities and capabilities of use.

Protected combat

The hull was designed following guidelines that combine increased inclination in the front part with completely vertical sides that follow a similar configuration to the turret.

Through the combination of armor plates with ballistic fibers, a very resistant vehicle has been configured to face normal contemporary battlefield threats; a fact that is complemented, favorably, by an automatic fire extinguishing system and with a filtered air system that protects the transported personnel from aggressive nuclear, biological or chemical weapons.

The general distribution was designed to place the turbo-diesel Scania DS14 550 HP engine on the right front side, coupled with an automatic Perkins X-300-5N transmission. Such elements increase the frontal impact resistance and can be easily maintained thanks to a large top door that facilitates the access of maintenance personnel to substitute the propulsion system in less than 15 minutes.

The driving compartment is in the right side, the main turret is behind both the driving compartment and the engine and includes places for the vehicle commander and the shooter. Eight seats for other soldiers are located in the personnel compartment where they can shoot their own arms thanks to two rectangular hatches situated above them; inside access is obtained through a rear ramp.

Its tactical mobility is very satisfactory, because it has a wheel system comprised of

RECOVERY VARIANT

Designed to sustain and carry out maintenance tasks associated to the CV 90 family, the CV 90 ARV combat vehicle is equipped with various specific means for assigned tasks, it does however, lack offensive armament.

LIGHT ARMORED VEHICLE

The CV 90105 armored caterpillar track can be equipped with various armed turrets with 105 mm low recoil guns, a weapon that provides enough firepower to face battle tanks in favorable conditions, thanks to its reduced silhouette and high mobility.

seven wheels, a front drive sprocket and a rear idler wheel, elements that are coupled with a suspension that combines torsion bars and shock-absorbers.

The tracks are designed to easily operate on snowy terrain, for which they are 55 cm wide and have a ground pressure of 0.49 kg/2, that in turn facilitates its movement on soft terrain.

Powerful armament

Due to the basic Bofors 40 mm gun, evolved from the anti-aircraft gun of the same company. The CV 90 can be considered the most powerful and able CV at the moment, which can face most future threats, as it can easily shoot down targets at a maximum of 4 km thanks to the use of a UTAAS aiming system developed by CelsiusTech.

This armament can reach 300 rounds per minute at its maximum firepower; it includes an automatic loading system that distinguishes between the different types of ammunitions and is fed by loaders that can hold up to 24 rounds for immediate use, to which 48 more in the turret and 168 in the magazine are to be added.

MOBILITY AND PROTECTION

The 550 HP Scania engine moves the CV 90 providing it with good agility on all types of terrain, which is reinforced by its advanced suspension that is partially covered on the sides by armored panels. These panels impede damage if the vehicle is reached by light arm fire or splinters from explosions.

The firing angle of between -8° and +35° permits both the destruction of land targets and firing at aircrafts. To carry out the first task, the use of APFSDS-T armor piercing type, 3P prefragmented programmable with distance-fuse and MP-T multiuse tracer ammunition is basic. The PFHE Mk2 rounds are used to destroy aircraft targets thanks to their distance-fuse that activates an explosive prefragmented charge.

The secondary armament has a mounted

ANTI-AIRCRAFT AND MOBILE

Taking advantage of the features of the Bofors L70 40 mm cannon, an anti-aircraft vehicle has been configured that has an exploration radar that warns the crew of the target range. The CV 9040 AAV can accompany the rest of the components of the family while being moved.

SURVEILLANCE AND RECONNAISSANCE

Configured with a turret in which different surveillance measures are integrated, a laser device for targets and optimized communications, the CV 90 FOV was designed for advanced surveillance teams to transmit to nearby troops significant data about the movements of enemy troops.

M39 configured with a medium 7.69 x 51 mm machine gun that is coaxially mounted on the main armament and with a 3,000 round reserve for immediate use, two 71 mm Lyran illuminant grenade launchers mounted on the turret and two triple GALIX sets of smoke and anti-personnel grenade launchers.

The two top hatches in the personnel compartment permit the unfolding of a Bill anti-tank missile system that is able to reach and destroy any of the tanks currently in service.

This element is transported on the inside of the vehicle and it implements combat capacity without requiring sophisticated guide systems in the turret because the main armament is independent of it.

VERY INCLINED GLACIS

The front part of the armored CV 90 caterpillar track's chassis is very inclined and optimized to stop impacts of all types of projectiles. Its shape favorably influences its stealthy characteristics and impede its detection by electronic and visual means.

Considered the first modern CV put into production, the Bradley caterpillar combat vehicle, used by the United States Army Infantry and Cavalry units, has been tested in combat given that two thousand of them were used in the Gulf War.

Its technical characteristics and excellent tactical use possibilities, accompanied by battle tanks in advance, were proven by the fact that only three of them were destroyed by enemy fire and the fleet reached an availability rate of over 90 %; a very high figure, if we keep in mind the inherent maintenance and operational difficulties caused by the arid climate.

A new combat concept

At the same time that the new Bradley M113 armored combat vehicle was being delivered to the army, the need for a more specific vehicle which possessed greater mobility, protection and firepower became apparent. In order to be on equal terms with other armored vehicles and tanks which were coming into service at the beginning of comming into service ar the beginning of the seventies.

Industrial requirement

The U.S.Army's proposal took shape in the form of a document in April, 1972, in which evidence of the necessity to introduce a new MICV was shown and that listed the basic features that it should have in order to face the challenges of the future. Many companies presented their proposals and, after many validation studies were carried out, the Chrysler Corporation, the FMC Corporation and the firm Pacific Car and Foundry were chosen. In November of the same year the Ordinance Division of the second company was awarded with the development of the engineering and the initial prototype production, a phase for which a 29.3 million dollar contract was signed.

In its clauses, the design, development and fabrication of three prototype vehicles, one vehicle for ballistic testing, 12 chassis for navigation testing and the building of the necessary elements for evaluation was contemplated. Under the name XM723, the prototypes were manufactured and armed with a 20mm cannon and delivered in the Summer of 1975 for testing.

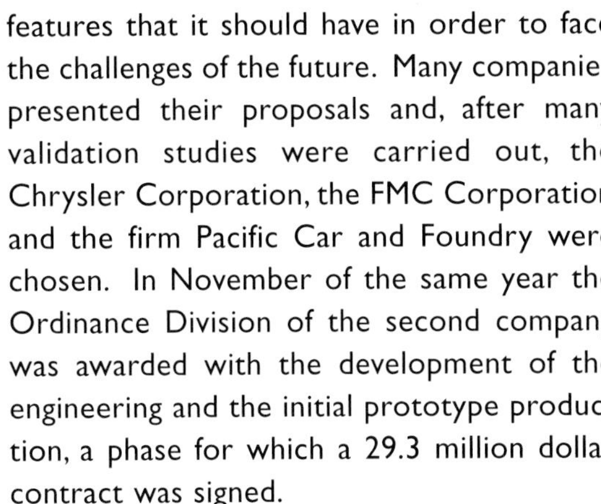

EUROPEAN DEPLOYMENT

The United States has, deployed in Europe, an important armored contingent to stop a hypothetical invasion from the East. Its arsenal is made up of several thousands of M2 Bradley vehicles specially camouflaged for operation in central Europe.

VERY FUNCTIONAL

The large quantity of Bradleys that lend their services to the US Army and the time gone by since their introduction, 18 years ago, has enabled its crews and technicians to learn all of its aspects in detail which influences favorably its functioning.

Conceptual changes

The tactical changes and technical advances achieved from the beginning of the program's conception, drove the evaluation commission to introduce a series of changes to the prototypes whose details were accepted by the Army in October 1976. Parallel to the original design changes, the name of the program was changed to the initials FVS (Fighting Vehicle System) and included the development of an Infantry variant (IFV), known as the XM2 and one for the Cavalry (CFV), called the XM3.

TECHNICAL CHARACTERISTICS OF THE IFV M2A3 BRADLEY

COST IN DOLLARS:	1,400,000
DIMENSIONS:	
Total length	6.55 m
Height	2.972 m
Width	3.61 m
Ground clearance	0.432 m
WEIGHTS:	
Prepared for combat	30,391 kg
Fuel	662 l

ENGINE:	
Cummins VTA-903T 14.8 liter diesel engine that yields 600 HP at 2,600 rpm	
FEATURES:	
Maximum speed	61 km/h
Range	400 km
Vertical obstacle	0.91 m
Fording	It is amphibious when prepared
Power/weight ratio	17.9 hp/t

The first was designed to transport a driver, the vehicle commander, an operator, the gunner and 8 soldiers and their equipment; while the second substituted the gunner and the soldiers with two explorers and more ammunition for the main armament. The first units with the definite configuration were built delivered to the Army for testing in December 1978, and finally accepted as the M2 and M3 in December of 1979.

Two months later the first order for 100 units was placed, charged to the 1980 budget; in May 1981 the deliveries began, and continued from then until February, 1995, at a variable rate that reached 700 units per year at its peak. In October 1981, it was decided that they would be called Bradley in honor of the accomplished General Omar N. Bradley. The last deliveries comprise 6,778 M2 and M3 vehicles, among which hundreds were built by Saudi Arabia and delivered between 1989 and 1993. To this which we must add two thousand modified variants to configure specialized vehicles like the MLRS rocket-launcher or the electronic EFVS support device.

SPACIOUS TURRET
The main turret stands out because of the availability of its elements. It has two armored hatches prepared with sights that allow the commander and gunner access to the inside of the vehicle, as well as exterior observation.

MAINTENANCE TASKS
In the Texas base of Fort Hood, and during a routine maintenance session, we can see some US Army specialist working on perfecting the Cummins VTA-903 engine of 500 HP, an assignment that has taken it (the engine) out of its compartment.

Made for survival

The introduction of this vehicle has motivated various disputes in the US Congress and Senate, in relation to its features and lack of protection. It was designated as a commission to verify and solve these more political than technical problems, given that the US Army still continues to constantly implement the capacity of its armament systems.

Advanced models

The delivery of the basic versions to the units —the first to receive it was the Second Division battalion in Fort Hood, Texas— and its acceptance through extended testing and exercises highlighted the need to substantially modify certain areas. After manufacturing 2,300 units of the variant A0 between May 1981 and April 1986, the introduction of the A1 was decided on which included the possibility of using TOW II anti-tank missiles and an improved fire suppression system. Up to April 1988, 1,371 units had been built.

The following month the A2's arrived from the production line with a boosted engine, enough protection to resist 30 mm impacts, interior Spall Liners to avoid armor chipping, changes in the ammunition magazine and preparations to improve future armor. 3,107 units were produced until February 1995, the date at which the initial modernization to this configuration began.

Its use during operation Desert Storm indicated that a series of improvements was required to the vehicles (visual protection from lasers, global placement system, counter-measures against missiles, etc.), that are now known as ODS. They were developed by the firm United Defense, the actual name of the manufacturer, as an updated version, known as the A3, to face the digitalization and threats of the 21st century.

INFANTRY AND CAVALRY

The US armored Infantry and Cavalry units have more than six thousand armored Bradley caterpillar tracks available to them that can battle in all types of conditions.

INTEGRATED MISSILE LAUNCHER

The left side of the turret of the M2/M3 integrates a bi-turbo retractable missile launcher from which long-range TOW II anti-tank missiles can be launched and five more can be stored in the personnel compartment.

Advanced and efficient

They are built from 5083 and 7039 type aluminum and include an armor plated and titanium panels fastened to the shell, which makes it resistant —according to the manufacturer— to 95 % of the weapons that are present on the battlefield today. The Bradley is configured with the driver located in the front left part, a central turret where the vehicle commander and the gunmen work, and a transportation section that is accessed by a big rear door where 6 soldiers are located —in the latest versions— that have individual seats.

The turret, made of steel and aluminum includes an advanced fire control system that combines optical and thermal sight elements, like the second generation infrared HTI finder, a McDonnel Douglas M242 Bushmaster 25 mm Chain Gun equipped with 300 rounds for immediate use and 600 more stored internally, a medium M240C 7.62 mm machine gun coaxial to the main armament and with a total of 4,400 rounds, a double launcher to fire TOW II anti-tank missile with room for a further five inside the vehicle and various complementary armament for the for the personnel being transported. Of the latter, a medium M60 machine gun stands out, 5,040 rounds for individual assault rifles and three disposable rocket-launchers.

As far as propulsion is concerned, we must point out that the last models have a Cummins VTA-903T engine that yields 600 HP, this is coupled to an automatic hydromechanical HMPT-500-3EC gearbox that provides for easy movement, although its specific power is reduced and its movements are a bit slower than other more modern models. The A3 model has an installed digital data bus that aids the connection of different subsystems and the linking of digital elements to their units to receive and transmit all types of data and to verify, with self-testing devices, different logistical parameters related to maintenance.

Similarly, the system that filters any NBC's from the external air and transmits it to indi-

USEFUL LIFE

After 18 years since its production started, the M2 and M3 series of caterpillar track vehicles will be kept in active service until the second decade of the next century, in which a new model will be introduced to complement the first and later substitute it completely.

vidual masks, is outstanding. The automatic fire suppression unit associated to Halon extinguishers and the EPLRS (Enhanced Position Location Reporting System) which enables one to distinguish the exact position of their own squad vehicles, in order not to destroy them in extreme conditions when it is difficult to identify the enemy.

Family airs

In 1977 the decision was made to implement the versions by developing a specific chassis that used common motive components and that could be adapted to various configurations, although at first it was intended to transportin the MLRS multiple launch rocket system which combines two cells for six rockets, or two modules for the ACTAMS missile.

Subsequently, other variants have been manufactured including a command and control vehicle with a protected container against aggressive NBC's in which the devices and servers and a fire support vehicle in charge of assigning targets are located. The Linekicker model to transport the Stinger anti-aircraft fire units, a version for engineering combat, a sanitary evacuation ambulance, a repair and maintenance vehicle, an electronic fighting vehicle system (EFVS), developed especially to transport the Crotale anti-aircraft system, a 120 mm mortar carrier and other systems are in the process of development.

These models follow the design guidelines started by the M2/M3 s, but they add an elongated chassis to the combat configuration that includes an increased number of elements in the suspension system. Along with that the stability is increased, the platform transport capacity is augmented and and

LAST MODEL

The armored Bradley M2A3 is the last variant of this model that United Defense has developed. Many improvements have been made to weaponry, command and control, survival, maintenance and mobility, as well as a central processing unit that links various subsystems through a data bus.

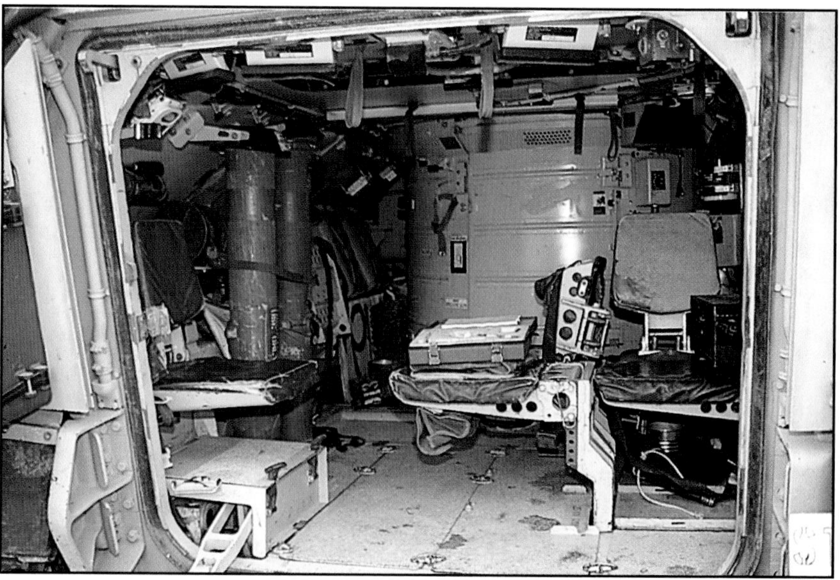

developed that —despite the time that has elapsed since the beginning of production— conserves very advanced characteristics that allow it to work together with battle tanks on any terrain and in any circumstance.

A new improvement program is planned for the Bradley family, which will integrate changes in its propulsion element. Its armament and protection will include the most advanced technology with regard to a lower consumption and increased engine power. A similar 35 mm mount that will be operated by a more advanced fire control system will replace the main gun. Likewise, new protection technologies will be implanted to diminish infrared beams and include ceramic and mixed elements, which will be able to face both direct and indirect impacts.

WHEEL SYSTEM

Configured with six roadwheel, an idler wheel and a drive sprocket, the suspension includes shock absorbers and torsion bars so that the vehicle —which reaches 30 tons in its latest versions— can move trouble-free on all types of terrain.

COMBAT TESTED

More than two thousand Bradley armored vehicles were deployed to Saudi Arabia during Operation Desert Storm. Its sand color camouflaged for desert operations and has side panels to implement its armor against enemy projectiles.

VALIDATION PROTOTYPES

The concept of the Puma wheeled armored vehicle is in the process of validating different 4 x 4 and 6 x 6 prototypes. The PT-9 seen in the picture has angular forms and advanced features that are influential for its acquisition.

With a long tradition of licensed construction of all types of armored vehicles, the Italian defense industry has taken an important step forward over the last two decades, after undertaking the development of an important range of products with advanced features.

This process, was led by the Defense Vehicles Division of the IVECO S.p.A. and the Divison Otobreda de Alenia Difesa (partnership called Iveco Fiat Oto Melara). This combination now market a wide range of products from the light four-wheel drive Puma armored vehicles, to the heaviest Ariete second generation battle tanks.

Productive self-sufficiency

The engine that has helped beth firms to produce a wide range of high performace vehicles (the IVECO MTCA V6 turbo charged diesel), has been a specific requeriment of the italian army for sometime. It is the policy or the Italian armed forces to use only engines that had been designed and manufactured by their own defence industry.

MOBILE AND AIRTRANSPORTABLE

The dimensions of the Puma wheeled armored vehicle 4 x 4 variant are reduced enough in size and weight to permit airtransportation by heavy CH-47 Chinook helicopters. This feature considerably increases its tactical mobility.

Supplies of space parts are readly avaiable, and that they are able to influence any modernization in the medium term because of this.

Advancing step by step

The productive experience of IVECO, which provided a wide variety of the Italian Army's light all-terrain vehicles and trucks of different weights, designed a light armored

four-wheel drive vehicle designated mod. 6634, known by the initials AVL (Armored Vehicle Light). The Italians, who signed a contract with them to develop an armored family that could fulfill an acceptable role on the modern battlefield, tested its features.

In 1988, as a consequence of this requirement, the first prototype of a range called Puma was developed. A second unit was delivered the next year, and three more of the final version in 1990. The evaluations it was submitted to gave good results, and the satisfaction of the Army was indicated by the development of six specialized versions with the same platform. These were anti-tank vehicles equipped with TOW and MILAN missiles, an anti-aircraft version fitted with the MISTRAL system, a mortar-carrier with a medium 81 mm gun, ambulance and a mobile control station version. Of all of these features, its low silhouette, the standardization of the majority of its equipment and its versatility are remarkable.

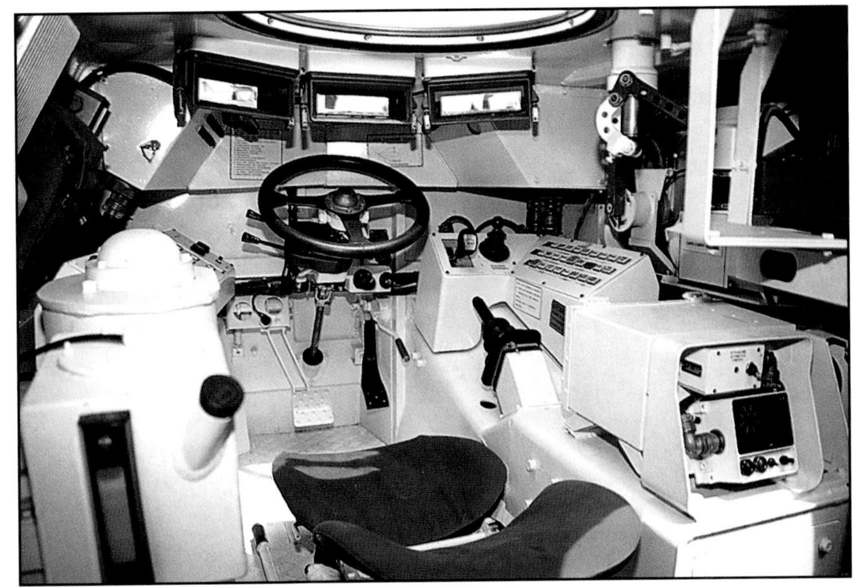

DRIVER'S COMPARTMENT

The driver's compartment of the Italian Puma wheeled armored vehicles is ample, ergonomic and thoroughly tested. These details will increase the driver's performance if he is comfortable and the controls are accessible.

The Puma is definite

The personnel carrier variant was given the general designation Model 6634G, it was decided to work on both the 4 x 4 and 6 x 6 design which have a greater load capacity. Both, fabricated with armor plated panels, designed to resist light armament fire, have a similar exterior configuration. With an angled top front part and flat rear —where the lights

HEAVY ARMORED VEHICLE

The Centauro, configured on an 8 x 8 traction armored vehicle platform, has proven to be agile and to have noteworthy combat features. It has already been deployed and used in Bosnia and Somalia by the Italians.

are located— there is a side access door on both sides and another in the rear. A central surveillance turret is located on the top part and can be substituted by a mount for various weapons and a hatchway in the personnel area, that permits both vision and the firing the soldiers' guns.

The 4 x 4 models have a weight of 5.5 tons, and a 7 person crew. Its dimensions are 4.72 m long and 1.67 m in height. The 6 x 6 version is a little larger; it weighs 7.5 tons, is 5.075 m long and the same height as the earlier version, and has an interior capacity for nine people.

Shared elements

Both vehicles are propelled by a 4 cylinder Iveco 8042 diesel engine developing 180 HP at 3000 rpm; the transmission is a German Renk.

The aforementioned propulsion group can reach a maximum speed of over 100 km/h, and can overcome gradients of 60 % and side slopes of 30%, and has a range of nearly 800 km.

The variants have been equipped with light anti-tank weapon fittings and medium MG-42/59 machine guns that can be mounted on both. Both models have seats for all personnel members, lateral smoke grenade launchers, clamps for support elements like pickaxes and shovels and a dynamic filtered air system integrated in the air conditioning unit to protect the crew members in the face of NBC's.

CONCEIVED FOR COMBAT

The Dardo caterpillar track combat vehicle was designed incorporating the latest developments in terms of mobility, firepower and protection in order to configure a combat element as capable as other already developed vehicles.

OUTSTANDING CONFIGURATION

The configuration of various elements of the Centauro allowed its quick introduction in the Italian Army, and the Spanish Army is expected to receive a total of 24 vehicles after the year 2000 for its Fast Action Forces (Fuerza de Acción Rápida).

Combat measures

To satisfy the combat needs of the Cavalry and Infantry units, specific models have been designed: the first is called Centauro and the second Dardo.

High mobility light armored vehicle

On the premise of having an armored vehicle able to reach high speeds on highways and therefore increase its strategic mobility, and one capable of easy movement on all types of terrain which incorporates fire control elements found in the Ariete tank and the CV Dardo, work was started in 1984 on the configuration of an 8 x 8 vehicle. Installed in it there will be a newly designed two-seater turret armed with a low recoil 105/52 mm cannon and the ability to fire a wide range of ammunition.

The first Centaur prototype was ready in 1987 and it was followed by eight more for testing. After checking its features, work began in 1990 to build four hundred of these armored, slightly modified units re-designated as B1's. Among its remarkable characteristics are its IVECO 6V 520 HP engine, its combat

weight of 25 tons, a hull length of 7.85 m, a maximum speed of 100 km/h and a four man crew.

The positive experience when it was used in Somalia and the former Yugoslavia, was fundamental to the Spanish Army's decision to acquire two dozen of them, has also motivated the initiation of development of the VBC variant for infantry combat.

Included is a turret with a 25 mm gun and 6 infantrymen can also be carried inside and an APC armed troop carrier with this will allow two more people to fit inside the vehicle.

Protection and mobility of the soldiers

In situations that require the Infantry to accompany the movements of the battle tanks to fight along side them, it is necessary to count on a high mobility CV with protection and adequate firepower. Keeping these criteria in mind, the engineers of IVECO began to work in February 1982, on the development of a new model, this was called the VCC-80 and after the building of three test prototypes, it was renamed the Dardo.

MAIN TURRET

The Dardo armored caterpillar track vehicle includes on its top part a two-seat turret armed with an Oerlikon KBA 25 mm cannon, a coaxial machine gun and two tanks for launching smoke and anti-personnel artifacts, each of which includes four launchers.

This vehicle follows along the lines of the others conceived in the last decade. Its best characteristics are the classic, high mobility hull, the same one as on the Centauro, and its great firepower due to its two TOW missile-launchers located on the sides of the main turret; it is also armed with a rapid fire Oerlikon KBA 25 mm gun.

Its stability, size, contents and other details allow it to be modified for configuration as a heavy 105 mm mortar carrier, a mobile control station, or a light armed tanks with a 105 mm gun.

Of its characteristics, the 23 ton weight and 6.705m, capacity to transport 6 soldiers and three crew members and reach a maximum speed of 70 km/h are noteworthy.

Production has not yet begun on this model due to lack of funds available in the Italian budget and the absence of export orders.

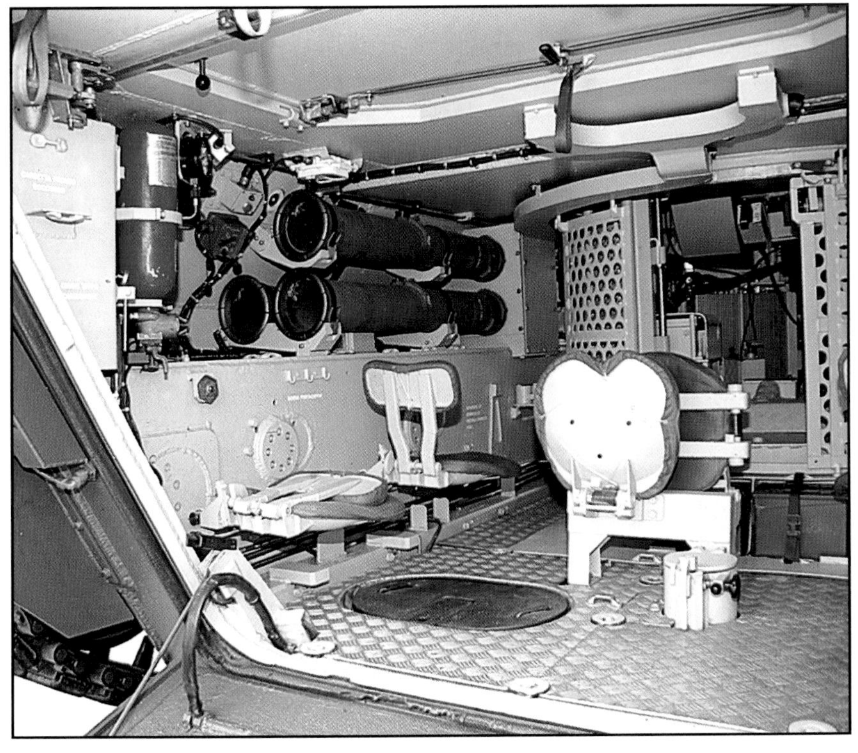

TROOP CARRIERS

The Dardo includes in its rear a compartment for transporting six fully-equipped soldiers and various firing elements, like the container tubes for the TOW anti-tank missiles.

SIGHT ELEMENTS

The illumination elements are located on the front part, on top of the upper glacis of the frontal area of the hull and consist of visible lights and war lights that make identification difficult in the case of night combat.

FIREPOWER

The two-seated turret of the Centauro VBC includes a main Oerlikon KBA 25 mm gun, a medium coaxial 7.62 mm machine gun, two mounts to launch long-range TOW anti-tank guided missiles and two banks for smoke and anti-personnel elements. associated with a sophisticated fire control.

ADVANCED ARMOR

Configured using armor plated panels, the front of the Centauro is characterized by a notable protection against all types of impacts, whether they be light guns or near explosions.

COMFORTABLE TRANSPORTATION

Two benches on the sides of the transportation compartment enable the infantrymen to travel comfortably, where they dispose of air conditioning and filtered air to improve traveling conditions until reaching the unloading point where the ordered task is to be performed.

REMOTE INFLATION

Each of the eight 14.00-20 tires that make up the suspension system are connected to a C.T.I.S. centralized inflation system that allows the time pressure to be adapted to the driving necessities on all types of terrain.

PROTECTION PANELS

On the sides of the Centauro VBC hull there are protection panels that avoid all types of impacts to the wheel system. They can be separated during transportation in which it is necessary to reduce its width and weight.

SIDE HATCHES

The hatches are located at the height of the transportation compartment on both of the sides of the Centauro VBC s wheel armory. They allow for exterior surveillance and shooting of the soldiers' assault rifles, thus improving the firepower of this mode of combat.

EASY ACCESS

The six or eight infantrymen that can be placed in the transportation zone of the Centauro VBC have a wide reinforced door available to them for quick and secure loading and unloading. The non-skid floor prevents accidental falls.

TECHNICAL CHARACTERISTICS

COST IN DOLLARS:	2,400,000
DIMENSIONS:	
Total length	7.932 m
Height	2.94 m
Width	3.280 m
Ground clearance	0.425 m
WEIGHTS:	
Combat loaded	24 t
ENGINE:	
IVECO MTCA V-6 turbo-diesel engine that yields 520 hp at 3,000 rpm	

ARMAMENT:

Automatic Oerlikon KBA 25 mm cannon with a reserve of 200 ammunitions, two medium 7.62 mm MG-3 machine guns, two anti-tank TOW missile-launchers and 8 80 mm grenade launchers.

PERFORMANCE:	
Maximum speed	+ 100 km/h
Range	800 km
Turn radius	9 m
Unprepared submergence	1.5 m
Power/weight ratio	21 hp/t

POWERFUL AND MOBILE

Some Cavalry Regiments have the VEC variants, equipped with a two-seat Hispano Suiza H90 turret with a 90 mm cannon that provides it the possibility to fire at targets situated at a distance of more than one kilometer and cause serious damage with its highly explosive shells and A.P. rounds.

The Spanish Cavalry and Infantry's motorized units of the Army share a thousand armored wheeled vehicles. These were manufactured and modernized by the national industry and were baptized by the deployed peace-keeping forces in the former Yugoslavia. On rugged terrain they were able to prove their strength and aptitude to carry out assigned tasks.

THOROUGH MODERNIZATION

Six hundred BMR's are going through an exhaustive updating process that consists of a new engine, implemented armor, changes to the combat and driver's compartment and other improvements, among which top rear supports for equipment and gear.

Contrasted needs

The situation of the armored park that the Spanish Army had at the end of the 1970's caused its senior representatives to study the introduction of a new armored vehicle model to be built by spanish companys.

A technical team was contracted to develop and plan the project and validate the different components, characteristics and features. The company Empresa Nacional de Autocamiones S.A. (ENASA) was chosen to carry out the manufacturing process.

Prototype validation

The first of the these vehicles, called Pegaso 3500 Armored Transportation Vehicle, was ready in 1974, simultaneously various tests were performed to check its features on all types of highways, roads and tracks in different locations in the peninsula.

The results recommended reducing its dimensions and, especially, its width which limited its mobility in some areas. This was done when other, smaller, Changes to the equipment location were made. Construction was to begin in 1976 with five preseries vehicles. These were given the name BMR-600 and were submitted to additional testing that lasted almost two years, at the end of which the vehicle went into mass production.

In 1979, the Military staff signed a contract with ENASA to accept the model and 245 vehicles of different variants, a process that was carried out in the company's plant in Valladolid that was known then as Pegaso.

Nine new versions are created

Along side of the testing of the new BMR, and as a consequence of the Cavalry units' manifested need, work was initiated to configure a specific vehicle to be used as a Cavalry Exploration Vehicle (CEV, VEC in Spanish). Due to the peculiarities of the mission it was to perform, and the armament that it was supposed to mount, a TC-20 two-seated turret with a 20 mm Rheinmetall gun, the exterior forms had to be reconfigured and the position of some equipment had to be changed, such as the engine, which had to be moved to the rear on the vehicle.

After being adopted as the VEC-625 and changing the main mount for an OtoBreda with a Bushmaster M242 25 mm gun, the deliveries began, and reached a total of 340 vehicles. Sixty of which were armed with the 90 mm Hispano Suiza H90 turrets that had been previously retired from the French armored Panhard AML-90 s.

MEDICAL EVACUATION

The BMR ambulance was deeply modified from the standard variant and is easily detectable from long distances because of the red crosses that identify it. It is a useful evacuation mean to bring injured soldiers in combat zones to areas where they can get medical attention.

INFANTRYMEN MOBILITY

The mechanized and motorized units of the Spanish Army have a thousand BMR vehicles which are used to transport soldiers to the intervention area, in other words, it's a safe mean of transportation to the combat zone.

The next to arrive were the variants created to perform specific missions, such as the BMR's that were modified as recovery vehicles with top crane and ground support elements, which stabilize it when on uneven surfaces, and a transmission center with different radio and communications systems located in the personnel transportation compartment. Mobile control station with auxiliary elements that facilitate operations of assigned subordinate units, engineers battle tank that includes a bulldozer blade on the front part and drilling equipment in order to lay mines, a evacuation ambulance with supports for stretchers and resuscitation equipment, mortar carriers with ECIA 81 mm and 120 mm guns, NBC reconnaissance, which required the re-designing and

expansion of the transportation compartment, anti-tank missile launcher with mounts for medium-range MILAN and long-range TOW missiles, both introduced in 1996.

CAVALRY EXPLORATION
The VEC-625 is configured to move small groups of soldiers at high speeds around battlefields. It is highly mobile and benefits from the 25 mm gun that allows it to face enemy vehicles that may discover the vehicle in action.

Sales success

At the same time that in 1988 the Spanish Army purchased 800 BMR's, work began on the Amphibious Mechanized Vehicle (VMA) that would equip the Armored Infantry Regiment of the Marines, a modified version in terms of the bow and the incorporation of systems to facilitate navigation from the amphibious fleets to the coast. A shorter, 4 x 4 variant was also developed, called the BLR, acquired by the Navy for its Regiments and Squadrons, by the Guardia Civil (military police) for the Grupo de Acción Rural (Rural Action Group), Equador and by the Air Force who uses it as an auxiliary means in surveillance and air base protection; the BMR's have been exported to Saudi Arabia, Peru and Egypt.

Classic design

This family of armored vehicles is configured with a high rigidity self-carrying shell made from welded panels of light ironclad pretensed aluminum alloy Al-Zn 4.5 Mg 1 that have a thickness and resistance against 7.62 x 51 mm armor piercing ammunition in the frontal arc and standard armored ammunition in the rest of the vehicle.

Ample configuration

Taking advantage of the previously mentioned configuration, a six roadwheel traction group was installed and four guide rollers coupled to an oleo-pneumatic high-absorption suspension that gives the vehicle stability on all types of terrain. The engine compartment is situated in the front right of the BMR and the rear in the VEC, which was were the Pegaso 9157/8 turbo-fed 306 HP engine was originally installed.

PROTECTED PERSONNEL
Close to one hundred BMR's were deployed in the former Yugoslavia within Spanish Groups.

The driver's compartment is located on the front left side, were he has remarkable visibility thanks to a bulletproof glass hatch. Behind him there is an access passage to the front part and situated in the back is the transportation compartment were there are two benches that can hold up to 12 soldiers or transport cargo of up to 2.5 tons. The internal configuration of the VEC is different and the driver is in a central position in regards to the vehicle's centerline. The solders can enter through a rear folding hatch door, they have two small hatches in the roof to see what is happening and fire support guns. The armament of the basic variant is a standard TC-3 turret that can be controlled from a protected interior position, a heavy Browning 12.70 mm machine gun that can fire at a rate of approximately 600 rounds/minute.

Modernization is approved

In order to solve some problems that came to light as a result of active use, in 1994 an industrial development phase was started to configure an improved BMR prototype and another VEC. SBB Blindados S.A, who have a factory in Las Canteras, Seville was chosen to carry out this process.

In the end of 1995, after testing its concepts, a contract of 19,380,000,000 pesetas was approved in which 646 vehicles were to be modernized in a process that lasted until 1999, the remaining vehicles were called M1.

The updating involves the incorporation of a hydrokinetic breaking system, changing the engine to a Scania, adopting Hutchinson puncture-resistant tires, reinforcing the most vulnerable areas with steel-plating of varied thicknesses, the incorporation of an anti-explosion Spectronix system associated to a Halon 1301 fire extinguishing system, and improving the driver's instrument panel. Various improvements on the hydraulic and pump systems, the incorporation of individual seats for transported personnel, a new heating and ventilation unit, changing the surveillance periscopes to the M-223A1, etc. These improvements have increased its operative abilities and reduced maintenance requeriments; this vehicle is expected to enter into service in the middle of the twenty-first century.

SECURITY ACTIVITIES

The armored BLR are used by groups and regiments of the Marine Infantries, a body that assigns it to security missions where it forms part of the deployment of protection for the Naval bases and arsenals.

FAILED PROTOTYPE

The VMA was developed from the BMR to configure an amphibious vehicle that satisfies the Marine Infantries. The bow has been greatly modified so it can navigate with ease. It is equipped with hydrojets for propulsion, although no series vehicles were acquired.

TECHNICAL CHARACTERISTICS OF THE ARMORED BMR-600

COST IN DOLLARS:	800,000
DIMENSIONS:	
Total length	6.15 m
Height	2.36 m
Width	2.5 m
Ground clearance	0.4 m
WEIGHTS:	
Prepared for combat	14,000 kg
Fuel	400 l
ENGINE:	
Pegaso 9157/8 306 HP engine in the process of being substituted by a Scania of similar specifications.	

FEATURES:	
Maximum speed	103 km/h
Range	1,000 km
Vertical obstacle	0.6 m
Unprepared fording	It floats and moves by its wheels or hydrojets
Power/weight ratio	22 hp/t

FIREPOWER

The Empresa Nacional Santa Barbara's TC-3 mount allows fire control of a medium Browning M2 12.70 x 99 mm machine gun from the interior of the vehicle without exposing the gunner, who can observe exterior actions through bulletproof sights.

COMFORTABLE DRIVING

The driver is situated in the front left part and has a complete instrument compartment that gives him the data of the engine parameters maneuvering the vehicle from the seat raised with his head exposed or through a thick glass bulletproof window that can resist 12.70 mm projectiles.

PADEL INCLINED

The aluminum elements that configure the front part are quite inclined to endow them with increased resistance against light weapon impact and shrapnel, having been reinforced with armor plates.

DIFFERENTIATING DETAILS

On the top part of the BMR's chassis is the engine's ventilation grille and two wide hatches for surveillance, firing, and evacuation. On the sides are the firing hatches, the smoke and anti-personnel grenade launchers and various complementary tools.

FIRING HATCHES

Some BMR's have side hatches, with bulletproof sights and a hole to place the assault rifle's mouth that allows the transported personnel to fire while protected by the vehicles armor.

RAPID UNLOADING

A rear door that is opened from the inside enables rapid unloading of the squadron that highlights a superior transport module with various logistics elements associated to tactical movements.

REDESIGNED INTERIOR

With the modernization of the M1, the BMR has redesigned its interior and the two benches have been replaced with individual seats and seatbelts to transport the soldiers more comfortably and safely on all types of terrain.

6 X 6 TRACTION

Mobility on all types of terrain is guaranteed by its efficient suspension associated with a hydropneumatic system; the front and rear wheels are steering wheels and the Hutchinson tires are puncture-resistant.

The M113, conceived to safely mobilize soldiers traveling inside, has become the most famous battle taxi in its class. More then 65,000 have been produced in the United States (not including vehicles produced under license) and they are still in service in a number of countries.

Easy driving and maintenance, satisfactory performance and economical operation are some of the features of this armored caterpillar track vehicle that has benefited in ample sales by the United States' Foreign Military Sales (FMS) which have promoted its exportation at reasonable prices, or at no cost due to the large number of vehicles that have been declared surplus by the US Army.

Born in the Fifties

The conception of this model was carried out in the middle of the fifties using, as a reference, military experiences of the Second World War and the Korean War, events that marked the need for multipurpose, light, highly mobile, all-terrain, armored airtransportable units that were also amphibious and could be launched with parachutes.

USED BY THE INFANTRIES

The Infantry units are supported by the different versions of the M113 for troop mobility and carrying out specific tasks. Its versatility and easy handling by highly trained personnel are its best features.

WORLDWIDE DIFFUSION

The technical characteristics, price and the number of vehicles produced has motivated diffusion of this US armored M113 caterpillar track vehicle around the world. It has contrasted reliability and a useful life that will allow many of them to remain active until the first decades of the next century.

Brief development

Its design began in 1956 and its development was performed by the FMC Corporation who verified armor plated and aluminum shielded prototypes.

Manufacturing began on the latter, initially known as T113 and later renamed as the M113,

at the beginning of 1960 at the San José, California factory, although a modified version fitted with a diesel engine to extend its range and eliminate the risk of fire was quickly put into production in 1963; this became known as the M113A1.

As soon as the vehicles reached the US units they replaced a large number of other older examples. Its best points are versatility and easy configuration to all versions necessary, which eventually reached around fifty. In 1978, when more than 25,000 vehicles had been produced for the US Army, the revised M113A2 model was introduced. Important changes made to this model were the suspension and air condicioning system.

The last model to arrive to the United Defense LP production lines —the producer's name changed with time— was the M113A3, whose production began in 1987; the last vehicles were manufactured in 1995 to fulfill an order placed by Kuwait.

Long production

Vehicles for troop transportation, evacuation, command units, recovery vehicles, engineer combat, mortar carriers, heavy anti-tank missile launchers, mine clearing, anti-aircraft Chaparral missiles or ADATS, cargo transportation, anti-aircraft Vulcan gun defense, detonation of explosives, battlefield reconnaissance, artillery surveillance, mine laying, air and land target detection, vehicles for OPFOR forces, that simulate a Soviet BMP-2, developed both by the manufacturer and its former users –converted the M113 in the most versatile military armored vehicle in the world. This variant is the most versatile model of those currently in world army arsenals.

Apart from the 65,000 vehicles produced in the US plant, many were built under license in other countries. 4,500 were made in the Italian OtoBreda factory, 500 in Belgian Mechanical Fabrications and more than 1,000 in the Korean Daewoo firm. This vehicle has been easy for many countries to purchase because of its low price and reduced development costs. Among its main users are: Argentina, Brazil, Cambodia, Canada, Denmark, Egypt, Germany, Iran, Libya, Morocco, Pakistan, Portugal, Somalia, Spain, Thailand, Uruguay and Zaire; the list of users contains close to fifty nations.

ENGINEER MODEL

The Spanish Army has modified dozens of its M113 vehicles to VCZ (Sapper Combat Vehicles) that have an incorporated bulldozing blade on its front part, supports in the top area, tanks for mine storage and interior devices.

MOBILE CONTROL UNIT

A specific M577 variant was designed to mobilize control units. The transport area is elevated to allow soldiers working there, with maps and tables and communications devices to have greater comfort. Usually many of them work together to carry out assignments.

Basic characteristics

The M113 follows a simple design concept, which causes its shape to be widely known around the world. It has been used in many conflicts around the world (it is typical to see images of U.S. soldiers riding on it in the Vietnam War), the M113 has stood out more from the rest because of its simplicity rather than its features.

Protected transportation

Made out of an armored aluminum shell with straight walls and inclined front, the conception of this caterpillar track contains an engine situated in the right front part and can

TECHNICAL CHARACTERISTICS OF THE M113A3 ARMORED CATERPILLAR TRACK VEHICLE

COST IN DOLLARS:	**690,000**	**ENGINE:**	
DIMENSIONS:		Detroit Diesel 6V-53T 6 cylinder 275 hp at 2,800 rpm	
Total length	5.3 m		
Height	2.52 m	**PERFORMANCE:**	
Width	2.54 m	Maximum speed	65.7 km/h
Ground clearance	0.43 m	Range	480 km
WEIGHTS:		Vertical obstacle	0.61 m
Prepared for combat	12,150 kg	Unprepared fording	amphibious, moved by the caterpillar tracks
Fuel	360 l	Power/weight ratio	22.29 hp/t

be accessed through a front hatchway; the driver is located in the front left part and has a specific cupola that enables him to drive the vehicle in a protected position; the commander is in the center where there is a mount for a heavy Browning M2 12.70 x 99 mm machine gun. A personnel transportation compartment is fitted with a bench on each side, a large folding door on the rear and a practical roof thanks to the two hatches with bulletproof glass.

Propulsion is carried out by the caterpillar track suspension system that is composed of five roadwheels, the drive sprocket and the idler wheel. The drive sprocket is coupled with a GMC Allison transmission that is powered by a Detroit Diesel 6V-53 6 cylinder engine. Driving is easy and carried out with levers that allow it to pivot on its axle and make quick changes of direction by braking one of the tracks. A noteworthy feature is its ability to overcome gradients of 60% and to cross trenches of 1.68 m. Its complete air/water-tight design allows it to forge waters at a speed of 5.8 km/h thanks to its tracks. A folding blade located in the front functions as a breakwater in navigation and is highly useful.

Optimized for battle

In Israel, France, United States and other countries, variants with increased features

LIGHT ARMORED VEHICLE

The versatility of the M113 platform can be easily and efficiently configured to various specific models for anti-tank battle. We can see, among these, the Spanish vehicles modified to place the MILAN system launcher on a superior mount and transport reserve tubes inside.

IMPROVED VARIANTS

Starting from the basic model, improved variants in terms of mobility, firepower and protection have been developed include this AIFV, fabricated by the Turkish Nurol company under the FMC license. It is has a cost much lower than a last generation CV.

for combat have been developed. Many of them have risen out of military needs manifested occasionally by their participation in low intensity conflicts were its walls have proven effective in stopping only projectiles fired by light guns. This evolved concept was followed by models like the United Defense MTVL (Mobile Tactical Vehicle Light) that has been elongated with another roadwheel in the caterpillar track. A 350 HP engine is included which has an armor plate kit that is fastened to the aluminum 5083 shell with bolts in the case of conflict, thus providing the vehicle with the capacity to resist 30 mm armor piercing projectile impacts in the front arc. The more advanced AIFV (Armored Infantry Fighting Vehicle) were designed starting from the basic model which had been heavily modified. Belgium, Holland, Philippines and Turkey have adopted these vehicles because of their thick rolled armor plates fastened to the front and sides of the shell. The transportation area was also redesigned with inclined walls on which hatches were added to facilitate the firing of their own guns by the seven infantrymen that fit inside. Its features were improved with the possibility of installing a one-seated armored turret with a 25 mm gun which provides increased power to support the infantry's advance; its weight is a little over two tons more than the basic vehicles.

MULTIPLE CAPABILITIES

The transportation compartment, located in the rear 2/3 of the M113 caterpillar track vehicle, can be configured for different functions of which its mobile control compartment reflects the detail of this American vehicle.

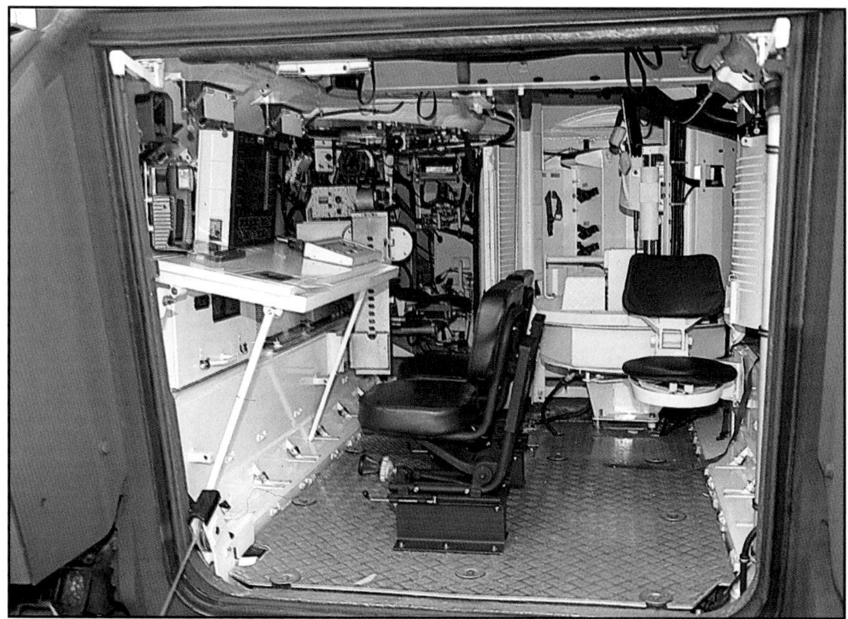

Evolved versions

Military necessity or intentions to sell to other countries has driven many companies to undertake a project to transform the

M113 into a more advanced, vehicle. Among the many possibilities available on the market, the Italian Alligator is noteworthy because of its peculiar characteristics that have substantially changed the front of the vehicle. The amphibian LVTP-7 incorporates a complex system moved by hydrojets at the rear that enable unrestricted navigation, even in the sea. The Spanish SEM-II, with a mine lay configuration variant in the cargo area like the M548 transportation variant, has a module with a plow, automatic transmission and control device with which anti-tank mines can be laid quickly and effectively. The Israeli Togas consists of a large armored box situated on the vehicle to increase protection against projectiles of up to 14.5 mm. The M113, modified by Vietnamese army technicians using Soviet engines and armament, employs many of the developments neglected by the United States after abandoning the area in 1975. The Canadian Lynx reconnaissance variant is much shorter and lower to hinder location; the German GA version has the rear area modified so that the queen archer radar system can be installed. This system is used to trace the parabolic traces of projectiles and motor rounds so that the location of the firing position can be determined exactly.

MORTAR CARRIER VARIANT

In order to mobilize mortars, whose fire curve establishes launching position, and to avoid enemy counterfire, medium and heavy mortars are placed in the cargo area of this armored vehicle.

RECOVERY VEHICLE

Some M113A2 have been modified to the recovery variant which includes a crane and an interior hoist to ease the recovery of other obstructed vehicles. It can also be used as a support vehicle for other tasks.

PROTECTED TRANSPORT

The TPZ-1 is a 6 x 6 wheeled armored vehicle widely used by the German Army, as a personnel transportation variant and other more specific variants that include electronic war, reconnaissance in NBC contaminated areas and cargo transportation.

The need to maintain a great number of motorized and exploration units active, made the German Army initiate a process of incorporating large quantities of wheeled armored vehicles, some of which can still be found in service.

Currently, in order to complement and substitute them in the near future, work is being done on the conceptualization, design and development of various families of high quality vehicles to form an adapted offer that can comply with the requirements of the next century.

Weapon reconnaissance

In 1964, the German Defense Minister examined the requirements that the new family of military vehicles would have to fulfill in order to be developed during following decade. Among them were armored 4 x 4, 6 x 6 and 8 x 8 vehicles assigned to reconnaissance and transportation units which were to be equipped with as many common components as possible, and at the same time should be of commercial origin.

Work is started

The Joint Project Office was formed in 1965 with the idea to undertake the enormous project. Both representatives of the military world (future users) and companies that could be involved in the production took part. This group consisted of Büssing, Klöckner-Humbolt-Deutz, Friedrich Krupp, MAN and Rehinstahl-Henschel, and later Daimler-Benz.

The first job undertaken was the design of an armored reconnaissance vehicle that had 8 x 8 traction and an amphibious capacity. Nine prototypes were built and tested between April 1968 and the end of 1971. Rheinstahl Wehrtechnik —currently known as Thyssen Henschel— was chosen to build 408 vehicles designated as Luchs AARV (Armored Amphibious Reconnaissance Vehicle). These were carried out between May 1975 and the beginning of 1978.

As a result of the same effort a 4 x 4 variant, called Transportpanzer 2, arose and a 6 x 6 known as the Transportpanzer 1. Of the latter vehicle, 1,200 units were built for the German Army who named it the Fuchs and received the last vehicles from the first order in 1986. Other vehicles of this model have been exported to Israel, Turkey, Holland, Great Britain and United States, countries that received modified vehicles like NBC

TECHNICAL CHARACTERISTICS OF THE ARMORED VEHICLE 8 X 8 GTK

COST IN DOLLARS:	3,000,000 to 4,000,000
DIMENSIONS:	
Total length	7.88 m
Height	2.99 m
Width	2.592 m
Ground clearance	0.504 m
WEIGHTS:	
Empty	28.5 t
Prepared for combat	32 t

ENGINE:	
Turbo-diesel commercial origin engine with 600 HP	
PERFORMANCE:	
Maximum speed	103 km/h
Range	1,100 km
Vertical obstacle	0.8 m
Gradient/side	
Slope	60/30 %
Power/weight ratio	18.4 hp/t

COMPACT ARMORED VEHICLE

The Fennek, built together by the German Wegman & Co and the Dutch SP Aerospace & Vehicle Systems, is a highly protected armored reconnaissance vehicle prepared with advanced equipment that facilitates assignments given to its crew members.

reconnaissance vehicles or the EW electronic war variant; on the other hand, Venezuela and Saudi Arabia bought the basic variant.

Differentiating characteristics

While the first vehicle is busy performing weapon reconnaissance tasks, the second is basically an armored transport to bring troops to the combat zone. Consequently, the Luchs was developed with 8 x 8 traction that enables increased agility thanks to its 390 horsepower of its Daimler-Benz OM 403 engine; it has an integrated turret with a Rheinmetall Rh202 20 mm gun that can respond to enemy fire; it includes a 500 liter fuel tank that provides the vehicle with a remarkable range of over 700 km; its crew is made up of four soldiers.

This armored vehicle, measuring 7.743 m in length and 19,500 kg in combat weight, was optimized to the A2 variant by the introduction of a thermal vision compartment and studies are being done to possibly implement its armor with additional plates since currently it only resists impacts of 20mm in its frontal area and turret. Also, the radio operator is in charge of driving operations when they are travelling in reverse, and is also completely amphibious and propelled in water by to two Schottel type tubed propellers with a propulsion speed of 10 km/h.

CARGO CAPACITY

The ACV truck was designed to transport personnel and materials; the former are situated in an armored front cabin with a six-man capacity and the latter in a rear area covered with a canvas that can withhold up to 1,500 kg of varied equipment.

In regards to the Fuchs, it should be pointed out that it is a different line of wheeled armored vehicles because the driver and the

commander travel in the front area; behind them is the Mercedes-Benz OM 402A engine that provides 320 HP at 2,500 rpm. In the rear we find the troop or cargo compartment that is 3.2 m in length, 2.5 m wide and 1.25 meters high. Either a maximum of 10 soldiers or two tons can be transported inside.

PROTECTED TRUCK

The ACV project is the result of a totally armored design for the Unimog light truck that grant this unit the possibility of being used unrestricted in peace keeping missions in which it is prepared for foreseen threats.

Its combat weight is 17,000 kg and many specific variants have been configured, like the one that transports Raist land radar detectors, the command and communications variant, the vehicle that corresponds to the Helas electronic war system and the one for detonation of EOD explosives of the German Air Force.

Future programs

German defense industries, especially those that work on the building of land armament, continually research new projects and develop increasingly more advanced models.

Vehicles have been worked on like the Lohr RPX 3000 or the Thyssen Henschel TH200, 400 and 800, to name a few.

Military needs

The increasingly technological needs of the German Army, with aspirations to contribute in all types of military intervention or pacification operations, have pushed for new

ARMORED CABIN

The ACV truck cabin is completely armored and the vehicle's engine has front ventilation grilles that protect it from all types of impacts. The interior is accessible through two side doors.

COMPLEMENTARY PROPULSION

The 6 x 6 TPZ-1 armored wheels are equipped with two propellers in the rear part, on the sides of the loading door, that allow the vehicle to propel itself in water and to navigate easily at a low speed.

products to be designed, among which the Fennek reconnaissance vehicle or the ACV truck (All-protected Carrier Vehicle) are included.

The design and development of the first vehicle is shared between the German firm Wegmann & Co. and the Dutch SP Aerospace & Vehicle Systems due to the interest of both countries in its development. The testing of the prototypes has gone well and manufacturing is scheduled for, at least, three hundred of them. Its high mobility 4 x 4 chassis and great agility provides the 250 HP engine with a very low consumption and the ability to travel 900 km without refilling the tank; its low silhouette also makes it difficult to locate by the enemy.

The Fennek weighs 9.7 tons, has three crew, a 40 mm automatic grenade launcher, a medium or heavy machine gun and an integrated satellite global positioning system. This enables it to know its position to within 10 m. For surveillance it is fitted with a hydraulic mast, on top of which there are various sensors including a daylight television camera, a thermal intensifier and laser rangefinder.

As far as the ACV is concerned, it is manufactured by Krauss-Maffei in its Munich factory and has a 4 x 4 Mercedes-Bebz Unimog 1550L truck chassis that is fitted with a completely airtight central cabin with bulletproof glass in which six people can travel.

In the rear part there is a small loading area that can hold up to 1,500 kg of equipment. Its weight reaches 8.8 tons and its maximum speed is 110 km/h. It is very useful

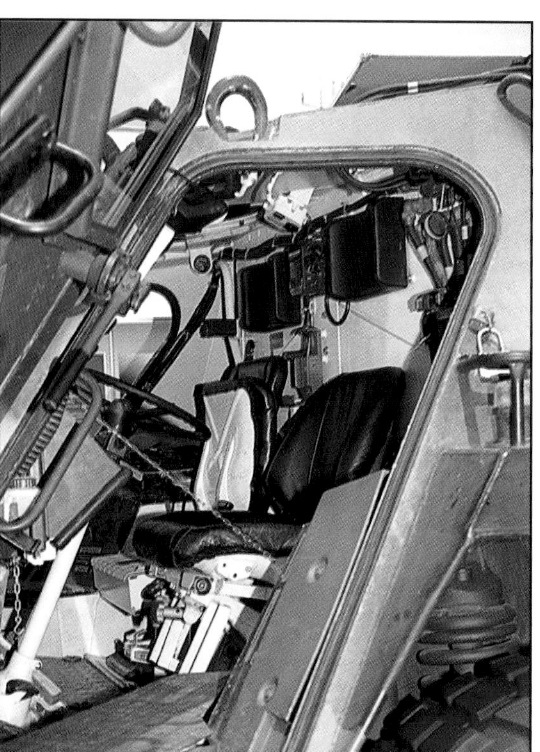

DRIVING COMPARTMENT

Breaking the general scheme of the majority of wheeled armored vehicles, the TPZ-1 includes a front cabin where the driver and the commander are situated that have individual side doors available (see left photo).

ADVANCED RECONNAISSANCE

On the top of the mast, located on the Fennek armored reconnaissance vehicle, a stabilized remote control module is located which has a daytime television camera, a thermal channel for night use and a laser rangefinder to know the exact distance to the target or observed point /see right photo).

for missions such as putting troops in positions were there is the risk of receiving heavy incoming fire or for crossing mine fields.

Multinational armored vehicle

The more advanced multinational project GTK (Gepanzertes Transport-Kraftfahrzeug) is being carried out by joint companies in France, Great Britain and Germany —Mak, Wegmann and Krauss-Maffei being the German representatives. This advanced armored vehicle has 8 x 8 traction, although the production of a 6 x 6 is foreseen; it is a modular concept which is being developed with clear growth options, especially in the adoption of complementary armor that increases its resistance against high intensity threats. It has a 600 horsepower engine, weighs 32 tons when prepared for combat, is 7.78 m in length, its maximum speed is 103 km/h and its range is 1,100 km.

Its configuration is remarkable, with a sort of modular tractor fabrication that has a fixed structure with a front cabin for the driver and the driving group. The wheel chassis a fitted with eight wheels connected to double shock-absorbers and torsion bars, to overcome more difficult terrain, depending on the mission it has to perform. An armored module can be fitted in which eight soldiers can travel with combat equipment and an integrated weapon system on the top part. Currently, it has from simple automatic grenade launcher mounts to single-seat turrets equipped with 30 mm automatic guns.

MULTINATIONAL PROJECT

The GTK armored troop carrier is a project that involves specialized industries from Great Britain, France and Germany. It is noteworthy because of its size, weight and possibilities when faced with threats that may be presented in the next century.

The never-ending possibilities for change or growth provided, will facilitate the development of specific groups to carry out other functions by only building one special design for the transmission, command, anti-tank combat with missiles, anti-aircraft defense with gun or missile mounts, recovery, etc. This way, a fleet of vehicles based on the same platform has many possibilities, depending on the tactical situation. This solution allows lower purchasing costs, and a greater number of vehicles of a given type to be available for a given situation while at the same time it provides for greater manteinance viability.

MULTINATIONAL ARMORED VEHICLE

The need to attain a low silhouette compact armored vehicle assigned to surveillance and reconnaissance tasks, has driven the German and Dutch governments to work together on its development, a task that will be shared also in production.

DESERT LIGHT ARMORED VEHICLES

The Vextra 105 armored vehicle has been thoroughly tested by the United Arab Emirates. Its 6 x 6 traction the high capacity of its fuel tanks and its ideality for non-stop combat in difficult desert terrain are proven. It, at the same time, reaches high qualifications when tested for firepower.

The geo-political position of France, which has business interests worldwide and former colonies which follow the economic directives laid down by Paris, has placed France in third position of countries that export weapons.

To maintain and increase their presence in the world arms market, they have maintained a powerful military industry which undertakes the production of the most varied weaponry systems and has a worldwide reputation. Of their companies, who are dedicated to the manufacturing of land armament those that produce various armored wheeled vehicles used all over the world it should be pointed out, GIAT, Panhard, Acmat, Creusot-Loire and Renault are of the most significant ones.

FUNCTIONAL PROTOTYPES

GIAT Industries is developing an 8x8 armored Vextra that combines an advanced platform with a TML turret prepared with a 105 mm gun and a stabilizing system that allows firing at all types of targets while in motion.

French requirement

In 1978, the French Army sent out a proposition to provide a light armored vehicle that weighed no more than 3,500 kg. That could perform both anti-tank and intelligence collection and reconnaissance; this vehicle was called the VBL (*Véhicule Blindé Léger*).

4 x 4 light vehicle

After carefully studying the proposals of five companies and granting contracts for the construction of three prototypes and the testing of two of them. The proposal from the reputable Constructions Mécaniques Panhard et Levassor, known worldwide as Panhard, was accepted in 1985.

The fifteen prepared VBL's were delivered to the army in October 1988 and were submitted to all types of tests, especially in difficult conditions that included their deployment within the Lebanese pacification contingent. Earlier, an order of 569 vehicles was placed, and delivery began in 1990 and was followed by others, thus making a current total of more than 1,100 vehicles.

The adoption of this small armored vehicle, the export variant is called Ultrav, has awoken the interest of many countries that, like Spain, have thoroughly tested it for their reconnaissance and cavalry troops. Forty of them have been acquired by the Mexican Army and smaller lots by Cameroon, Djibouti, Gabon, Niger, Portugal, Rwanda, Togo and Qatar. This vehicle was designed to perform quick, discreet movements in all types of conflicts. Its best basic characteristics are four wheel drive traction propelled by a Peugeot 95 HP engine associated to an automatic gear box, armor structure made from armor plates between 5 and 11 mm thick and thick bulletproof windows, two side doors and one rear door for easy interior access, a practical turret on the top part on which various systems for light weapons or intelligence collection can be installed. Likewise, its low noise level makes it more difficult to locate for enemies.

Transportation family

Larger than the other, and designed initially for personnel transportation, the VAB (Véhicule de l'Avant Blindé) is offered by GIAT industries in 4 x 4 and 6 x 6 variants. This model, conceived by the Saviem/Renault group in the beginning of the 1970's, adopted in May 1974 by the French Army and produced between 1976 and 1993 during which time 5,000 vehicles were produced. It was similarly acquired by Morocco, Qatar, United Arab Emirates, Brunei, Cypress, Lebanon and Oman.

PROTECTED ADVANCE

The mobility and protection that the armored VAB provide to transported troops is ideal to guarantee its advance toward combat zones. This way survival is guaranteed to the transported personnel even when hit by light gun impacts or grenade and howitzer splinters.

The 4 x 4 wheeled armored VAB's are in service in various functional units assigned to rapid deployment, like this vehicle used for the Marine Infantry troops to consolidate their advances to the beachhead.

The majority of the four thousand vehicles that the French use are 4 x 4's in which the driver, commander and heavy 12.70 mm machine gun operator and ten soldiers travel. The shell is made from steel that is air/water tight enough to navigate supported by two propellers situated in the rear and the front blade which acts as a breakwater. It is 5.98 m long, weighs 13 tons an is propelled by a Renault MIDS 06-20-45 turbo-diesel engine that produces a maximum of 220 hp; enough to move it at a maximum of 92 km/h and to allow the transportation of various armament configurations such as the GIAT turret with a 20mm cannon or systems like the RATAC location radar.

The 6 x 6 has the same length and motor as the former vehicle but it weighs 14.2 tons and was developed to provide a more stable platform to those specific versions that require better traction due to the weight they have to carry. Among them is the anti-aircraft vehicle with a double tube Dassault Electronique mount, the HOT system anti-tank vehicle, the VMO internal security system and the recovery vehicle.

Functions with a future

The wide number of armored vehicles sold by the French, many of which were of older models and many others that were not redesigned, among which are the AMX-10RC with a 105 mm gun, the VBC 90 of the same caliber gun used by the French Gendarmerie Nationale and the ERC Lynx exported to Mexico, have been fruitful generating a technological capacity in use today for next-generation designs.

Vextra 105

Designed as a means capable of facing battle tanks or being used in peace keeping missions, the armored Vextra stands out from the rest because of its 8 x 8 traction and because of its armament capacity. Its suspension system gives it excellent stability and enables it to reach more than 120 km/h and a range of 1,000 km, characteristics that were tested in the United Arab Emirates in the end of 1997.

Its armament is comprised of a TML two-seated turret equipped with a G2 105 mm low pressure gun and a technological fire control used on the Leclerc tank. Both elements allow it to fire at both still and moving targets during the day or at night within a radius of 2.5 km. The aiming system was built by SAGEM who also supplies the commander's panoramic surveillance sight and artillery fire control, both stabilized.

FIREPOWER AND MOBILITY

Armored 6x6 AMX-10RC vehicles combine a high mobility platform and a two-seat turret armed with a 105 mm gun that is capable of confronting tanks and other armored vehicles.

FUNCTIONAL EXPERIENCE

France has deployed its troops on various occasions to African and Middle Eastern territory, hard terrain in which the wheeled VAB armored vehicles have proven their mobile capacity.

Multinational and european

The British firms Henschel, Vickers Defence Systems and the French Panhard are working in collaboration on the design of

a new model with 6 x 6 in-line traction and advanced features. The characteristics currently known (we must not forget that this is a project in process and may change), are length of 7.12 m of length, the optimized transportation area for eight soldiers in a space of 1.15 m^2 that includes side harnesses for auxiliary equipment, it can transport 5 tons of cargo and has a main armor associated to Mexas sub-armor.

The propulsion group will consist of a 500 HP engine and an associated transmission of commercial origin, so as to avoid inherent development costs; the suspension will be of the active hydro-pneumatic type; the brakes will have ABS to optimize its capacity, and the tires will be inflated by a centralized device in the driver's area which is optimal for adaptation on different types of terrain.

An 8 x 8 traction variant of 7.53 m in length and a volume of 15 m^3 has been developed that can transport cargo of more than ten tons and will have a 600 HP engine.

INDUSTRIAL DEVELOPMENT

The French Panhard firm, in collaboration with the British and Germans, is working on the development and conception of a new family of wheeled armored vehicles known by the generic name VBCI.

COMPACT AND POWERFUL

The small AML-90 armored vehicles combine a very compact chassis with a powerful 90mm cannon. Its downfall is the reduced space available to the crew.

DRIVER ACCESS

An armored door is located on the right side of the VBL through which the driver can access the vehicle. He is in charge of communications operations, following maps, consulting information devices and helping the rest of the crew to carry out their tasks.

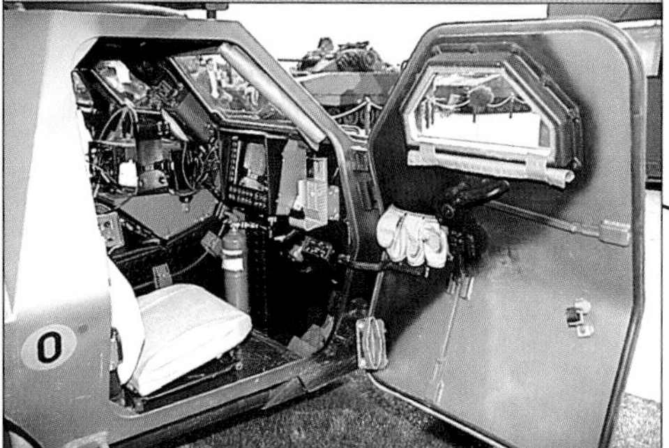

WEAPONS SYSTEM

On the mount located on the top part of this vehicle, various weapons systems operated by the third crew member can be placed. It can hold everything from a light machine gun to a medium-range MILAN missile-launcher.

PROTECTION AND EFFICIENCY

The armor shapes located on the front part give it an elevated resistance when faced with threats. It has an optional air filter system that allows it to combat in areas of aggressive NBC weapons. Its low silhouette and small size are remarkable.

DRIVER'S AREA

An armored side door with a Famas assault rifle mount to place the soldier's rifle on, allows the driver access to the driver's area of this light armored vehicle that has been optimized for comfortable and rational control and operation.

PROPULSION GROUP

The side ventilation grilles allow the small Peugeot XD 3T 95 horsepower turbo-diesel engine with 4,150 rpm to work which grants it a maximum speed of 95 km/h and a range of between 600 and 800 kilometers.

DIFFERENTIATING DETAILS

A big door is located in the rear that allows inside access to the third crew member in charge of operating the weapon systems that can be installed. The cased propeller allows navigation in calm waters.

COMPLEMENTARY EQUIPMENT

The exterior walls of the VBL are the ideal place to fasten auxiliary equipment like a pickaxe and shovel that can be used to get the vehicle out of difficult situations like mud or in swampy areas.

4 X 4 TRACTION

The four 9.00 x 16 wheels are associated o an automatic ZF transmission that has 3 forward and 1 reverse gear. The brakes are ventilated disks and the suspension is configured with torsion bars, shock-absorbers and helicoid springs.

TECHNICAL CHARACTERISTICS OF THE LIGHT ARMORED VBL-ULTRAV

COST IN DOLLARS:	**600,000**
DIMENSIONS:	
Total length	3.88 m
Height	1.7 m
Width	2.02 m
Ground clearance	0.37 m
WEIGHTS:	
Prepared for combat	3.55 t

ENGINE:	
Peugeot XD 3T turbo-diesel engine of 95 hp at 4,150 rpm	
PERFORMANCE:	
Maximum speed	95 km/h
Range	+600 km
Vertical obstacle	0.5 m
Unprepared fording	0.9 m
Power/weight ratio	26.76 hp/t

Conceived as a private industrial adventure by the firm MOWAG Motorwagenfabrik AG, located in the Swiss town of Kreuzlingen, different Piranha wheeled armored vehicles kept evolving until a very complete family was developed, of which more than 5,000 vehicles have been built in four different traction configurations.

In Canada, Chile and Great Britain, countries that have produced thousands of these vehicles under license, the Piranha has become the most successful wheeled armored vehicle in the last twenty years. It has been adopted by a dozen countries in which it has attained a notable reputation derived from its qualities and features proven over time in service.

PROTECTED MORTAR CARRIER

The stability and width of the 8x8 wheeled Piranha armored vehicle allows for various configurations of specialized versions among which this 120 mm mortar carrier is found and that includes, under the armor protection, ammunition stowage areas for the transported gun.

Development of the model

In compliance with the Swiss' own needs and to establish a good export reputation, the decision was made in 1970 to undertake the manufacturing of a 6 x 6 wheeled armored vehicle. The work took off quickly, the first prototype was ready in 1972 and the first produced vehicles began delivery in 1976.

The orders arrive

In February of the following year, an order for 350 units for Canada was confirmed, an agreement that brought with it the manufacturing, under license, by the firm Diesel Division of General Motors. This company has supplied the Canadian Army with thousands of Cougars, Grizzlies and Bisons and was in charge of the production of almost 800 of these armored vehicles for the United States Marine Corps (USMC). A small group of these vehicles have been transferred to the Australian Army, who evaluated them carefully and placed and signed an order with General Motors for a hundred more.

THE LARGER VERSION

Starting from the original Piranha design, various more modern and bigger variants have been undertaken. The 10x10 armored vehicle is longer and heavier than the models produced by the Swiss firm MOWAG.

At that time the production license was also granted to the Chilean company Cardoen Industries that produced 225 for the Chilean Army with the configurations of transportation units, mortar carriers, control units and combat vehicles. FAMAE is the company that now operates the project in Chile. At the beginning of the nineties, the British GKN Defence was authorized to manufacture it. A thousand vehicles were exported from Great Britain to Saudi Arabia (an order that also involved the Swiss and Canadian factories) and a few less than a hundred to Oman.

Orders from Sierra Leone, Nigeria, Ghana, Liberia and their own Army have been fulfilled directly from the Switzerland.

Classic shape

The first model to be configured was the 6 x 6 version that included a self-carrying shell made from welded steel that stood out because of its notable inclination in the front

and sides, a characteristic that implemented its resistance against all types of impacts.

With a generally classic configuration, its propulsion group is based on a 300 HP Detroit Diesel 6V-53T and an automatic Allison T-653 transmission with five forward and one reverse gear. Both are situated on the right side of the front part to increase protection and facilitate maintenance thanks to a large top grille. The driver sits on the opposite side and behind him the commander, who has his own surveillance hatch. The rear 2/3 are for the transportation of up to 12 soldiers.

MOBILE LIGHT ARMORED VEHICHLE

The Piranha platform in its 10x10 version is very useful to mobilize those heavy gun systems that need high stability during use, like this variant prepared with a 40 mm mount that can be used against air or surface targets.

Multiple configurations

Based on the 6 x 6 model that has a combat weight of 10.5 tons and is a total of 5.97 meters long, an ample family that includes a large quantity of specific variants and four different traction 2/3 models has been configured.

Mobility a la carte

The manifested needs of different countries are different in regards to the assign-

TECHNICAL CHARACTERISTICS OF THE PIRANHA III 6 X 6 WEELED

COST IN DOLLARS:	**1,200,000**
DIMENSIONS:	
Total length	6.25 m
Height	2.17 m
Width	2.66 m
Ground clearance	0.595 m
WEIGHTS:	
Combat maximum	12,000 kg
Fuel	200 l

PROPULSION:	
Detroit Diesel 6v53TA engine that yields 350 hp	
FEATURES:	
Maximum speed	100 km/h
Range	600 km
Vertical obstacle	0.60 m
Unprepared fording	1.50 m
Cargo capacity	3.000 kg or 12 soldiers including crew
Power/weight ratio	28 hp/t

ments these vehicles will be given. The smallest of the family is the 4 x 4 that weighs 7.8 tons prepared for combat, it has a Cummins 6BTA 159 HP engine in its original version and 210 HP in the more modern version. It was designed to be a low maintenance easy to use armored vehicle.

On the other hand, the 8 x 8 variants are more complicated to operate and maintain, although the advantage of its multiple traction provides it with better mobility and more stability. For this reason it is ideal for configuring combat elements and platforms associated to weaponry systems. The most updated variant, called the Piranha III, weighs 14,000 kg in the basic model and is equipped with a 280 horsepower engine. It is normal to see various armored turrets mounted on top or configurations from anti-aircraft defense systems to recovery elements.

The last to make it to the production lines was the 10 x 10, designed as a platform for heavy systems like a two-seat Cadillac Gage turret equipped with a 105 mm low recoil cannon and an automatic loading system, or as a logistics model that can carry all types of loads in the area previously designated for troop transportation. Its cargo capacity is 7.5 tons; its total weight is 20,000 kg, the engine yields 350 HP, can reach a maximum of 100

ARMED EXPLORER

The last 8 x 8 Piranha variant is the III model that includes a redesigned shell to more effectively protect the occupants and an armed turret with an automatic 25 mm cannon that provides it with high firepower in the face of any armed threat (see photo below).

THE MARINES' LAV

The US Marines Infantry uses almost eight hundred wheeled armored LAV's, of a Piranha variant manufactured in Canada that has proven to be very useful in both peace keeping missions and combat activities that require using maximum firepower.

However, the LAV-AD has been put into service. A dozen of these vehicles have been delivered, and they stand out because they include a complex anti-tank defense system with a low silhouette integrated on a Blazer turret that can turn a full 360°. Its anti-aircraft capacity is based on the combination of a multi-tube 20 mm gun able to fire 3,000 rounds per minute with a short-range Stinger infrared missile mount; a variant has been proposed equipped with the French MISTRAL missiles.

The wide variety of models used by the USMC and vehicle versatility are being kept in mind by the Spanish Marine Corps, who is contemplating the acquisition of these vehicles in its reinforcement plan for the XXI century, although it does not discard the idea of acquiring a tracked vehicle, like the Pizarro.

km/h and, despite its 7.20 m size, it can overcome gradients of 60 %.

The LAV of the Marines

The leaders of the USMC decided, in 1981, to complement their amphibious caterpillar track vehicle LVTP-7 with the incorporation of wheeled 8 x 8 armored vehicles that were called LAV (Light Armored Vehicles). The first on was delivered in October of the same year and equipped with a two-seat turret armed with a stabilized M242 Bushmaster 25 mm gun.

Its excellent performance during testing drove the USMC to acquire four hundred vehicles for soldier transportation during different combat phases; to these, various specialized models have been added like the LAV-R recovery vehicle, the LAV-L for logistics transportation, the LAV-M that has an 81 mm mortar in the personnel area, the LAV-C with command and control elements, the LAV-MEWSS with sophisticated electronic war devices, LAV-AT with a turret for TOW-2 anti-tank missile launching and a variant with a 105 mm low recoil cannon that has been studied in various configurations, but at the moment only one version has been built.

THE MOST VERSATILE

The 6x6 variant is characterized by its 9,500 kg combat prepared weight and 6.25 m length. The ample rear hatch facilitates loading and unloading of the troops; its redesigned shape bestows upon it greater resistance when faced with all types of impacts.

TABLE OF CONTENTS